RAISING THE DEAD

Raising the Dead

England's Unique Treasure

ARTHUR WRIGHT

Copyright © 2021 Arthur Wright

The moral right of the author has been asserted.

Apart from any fair dealing for the purposes of research or private study, or criticism or review, as permitted under the Copyright, Designs and Patents Act 1988, this publication may only be reproduced, stored or transmitted, in any form or by any means, with the prior permission in writing of the publishers, or in the case of reprographic reproduction in accordance with the terms of licences issued by the Copyright Licensing Agency. Enquiries concerning reproduction outside those terms should be sent to the publishers.

Matador
9 Priory Business Park,
Wistow Road, Kibworth Beauchamp,
Leicestershire. LE8 0RX
Tel: 0116 279 2299
Email: books@troubador.co.uk
Web: www.troubador.co.uk/matador
Twitter: @matadorbooks

ISBN 978 1800463 448

British Library Cataloguing in Publication Data.
A catalogue record for this book is available from the British Library.

Printed on FSC accredited paper
Printed and bound in Great Britain by 4edge Limited
Typeset in 11pt Aldine by Troubador Publishing Ltd, Leicester, UK

Matador is an imprint of Troubador Publishing Ltd

D.M. the genius that was my father.

Contents

1	The Treasure in the Crypt	1
2	Academic Night-Hawking: Where is the Tomb?	6
3	Measuring the Grave: The Problem of Lengths	10
4	Validation: Whose is the Body?	13
5	Who Made These Records?	16
6	Autopsy: What Do the Linear Units Record?	18
7	Why Both Linear and Areal Units?	20
8	Measuring the Bones: The Linear Units	23
9	Back to Basics: General Physiology	25
10	Woodlands	27
11	Pastures	30
12	Meadows	32
13	The East Anglian "Extents": More Than One Burial	34
14	Establishing Identity: Other Anomalies and Proofs	37
15	The Grave Goods: Mineral Rights	39
16	Summary: Ready Reckoner	41
17	Exploring the Tomb: The Areal Units	43
18	Controversy: Who Buried the Corpse?	46
19	The Solutions and Proofs: Waking the Dead	48
20	Reconciliation: Combining the Evidence	50
21	Subsequent Use of the Hide Unit: Voices of the Dead	53

22	Another Palimpsest: The Individuality of Kent	55
23	The Characters of Counties in 1066	58
24	Ploughlands	62
25	Could a Plough, Plough So Much?	65
26	Areal Units	67
27	Occluded Evidence: Other Land Uses	68
28	Swine Renders and Swinewoods	71
29	The Values of Woodlands	74
30	Sheep Pastures	77
31	Marshes and Fens	79
32	Validating the Evidence: Preferential/Beneficial Hidation	82
33	The Lesser Domesday A Senior Partner	89
34	Presenting the Case: Summary of Findings	94
35	From the Crypt of History: A Monster or a Priceless Treasure?	100

APPENDIX	Actual Linear Measurements	106
NOTES & SOURCES		111
INDEX		116

JUST 20 WORDS
IN TWO MILLION WORDS
WILL RAISE THE DEAD
BUT *WHERE* ARE THESE WORDS HIDDEN?

It has been described as "the most comprehensive array of social and economic data… possibly from the planet" – an historic object unique to England, a World Heritage as important as the Great Wall of China or the Pyramids of Egypt – yet Domesday Book has never been read.

It remains a 1,000 year old secret document and it is here, in England.

For over three hundred years scholars have translated and argued over it without knowing what it was saying. The "key" to decoding two million words and statistics actually rests in a single unit, it rests in a noun once common in England but unique in Europe, a unit which had an alternative name and an also unique name in Kent.

The riddle posed by this single unit buried in two nouns actually unlocks all the arithmetic this "book" contains. It certainly changes the English history we have always been taught. Incredibly it has defeated scholars time and again though it was clearly defined in the text all the time!

Twenty words in plain view that no-one could see though they were looking all the time! Twenty words which scholars and students "read", but they never knew what these words meant. Why? Because they had been told that they could not be read and so they surely had no meaning!

Just twenty words saying that "A + B = X + Y" and these were there in plain sight, the key to deciphering the entire document, but everyone preferred to believe what they had been told rather than what they could read. Here we have the antithesis of education and of scientific enquiry, a mistake equal to climate-change denial.

So this is the tale of a treasure-hunt for a priceless prize buried deep in the crypt of history, a search for a formula by which to end a millennium of secrecy, an archaeological discovery which was always there for historians to see yet one they could not read. They looked for the wrong thing because they expected something else.

Yet how, a millennium ago, could England have created such an astonishing archive? Read on, for the answer to this question is also in the answer to the riddle which was buried in the grave.

CHAPTER ONE

The Treasure in the Crypt

In equal parts disgusting and exciting – exciting alike avarice and repugnance – the sacrilege of opening a vault or tomb engages the imaginations and the doubts of all those who participate. Should it be done, why are we doing it and will "the curse of the Mummy's tomb" fall on those who dare to disturb eternal rest. Will the revulsion of the establishment inevitably fall upon the "nighthawks"? Yet what treasures, both intellectual and scientific, and maybe those of intrinsic value, lie within? Is the corpse still there, what can it tell us of its life and times, will it be sleeping alone? Surely it is because we wish to raise the dead that we are fascinated by history?

If we do this thing, whose doctrines will we offend, what laws of man or God will we transgress? What authority do we need, should we need, do we actually possess? The long process of gaining permissions or, alternatively, of planning the clandestine act may take us years of preparation for even the exact location may not be known. Will there be other bodies from later dates that overlie the one we seek? Has the grave been robbed before? That is an eventuality all archaeologists dread. Has the grave been reused? Such questions are a lure in themselves.

Among effigies and spectres, unseen and all around us, we now stand in a dark, damp and sinister subterranean space with spade and jemmy in hand, hesitating before taking the first, irreversible, step. Will public opinion, will posterity, applaud or condemn? We ask ourselves whether this is a crime scene, or are we committing a crime? Will some vengeful wraith, or perhaps even a living and guilty party, intervene? But then, there is still the temptation!

One of the cardinal Christian duties is to bury the dead, whatever their faith may have been, that is how this corpse came to be here, in the ground. Now we are going to dig it up, we are going to disinter the past and, either way, whichever way, it is a tale from the crypt. We are (many will say) treasure hunting. Should such things be left, decently buried? What price archaeology?

In this crypt is the promise of a treasure unique to England, a treasure not found anywhere else in the world, one that is rightly deemed fabulous. No sum of money could purchase it and, despite its great age, it remains intact, legible, it is capable of being read and reconstructed, capable of being resurrected. Surprisingly, no-one has done it yet! This is England's equivalent of the Great Wall of China or the Pyramids of Egypt and it takes the form of a book. How, a millennium ago, could England have created such an archive when no-one else in Europe could compile one, let alone accomplish it in perhaps six months?

> **"Domesday Book is the most comprehensive array of social and economic data... from anywhere in Europe, possibly from the planet" (ukdataservice.ac.uk)**

Very many books, let alone articles, have been written in order to "explain" Domesday Book and now we also have such "on-line" expositions, websites by learned academic sources. All these sources, it seems to me (I may be mistaken) claim to be able to "read" this incredible, this unique and amazing, archive, now almost one thousand years old, so how is it that <u>no scholar</u> can reconcile the statistics it contains with any internal evidence <u>or</u> with any more recent statistics? Which is not to say that some formidable analyses of these statistics have not been made, they have, but this failure tells us that no-one has yet managed to <u>prove</u> what these statistics might mean.

Many of these scholarly sources disagree with one-another, which is the proof that they are presenting opinions and not providing evidence. None of them can explain exactly what it says or (for that matter) why it was done. They can translate it but they cannot <u>read</u> it with any cogency and that is a fact. If reading includes logic, if it includes understanding, Domesday Book has certainly not been read!

In spite of superb translations and incredible efforts at analysis its testimony remains inaccessible, according to scholar after scholar. Yet the answers we seek as to the accuracy and values of the statistics it so comprehensively contains (within something like two million words) were there all the time. They are actually written large within this massive document. Although a "needle in a haystack" it was only ever necessary to read it carefully for all to be revealed!

Like any encryption, if you can find the "key" then, by applying it, the rest automatically unfolds and the system employed can be pieced together. Those in the past who read Domesday Book and studied it with more than usual care often came very close to succeeding, it has to be admitted but, time and again, they came up against academic rivalry (and, at times, jealousy) which curtailed their thinking. Researchers have, apparently, failed to pool and discuss findings outside accepted lines of thinking, what is now termed "group -thinking", and this prevented further progress. In my opinion, anyway, there has been too much formal teaching and not enough listening to the opinions of others.

"Arithmetical ingenuity", which is a common, "group-thinking", dismissal of all novel proposals, does not sufficiently explain the evidence contained and revealed within this present volume. Only statistical significance proves any methodology and you will find it <u>here</u>, thanks to the evidence left in their text by those who wrote Domesday Book. They left twenty words by which to inform future (authorised) readers, we might say future scholars, because, of course, Domesday Book was an official document and not open to just anyone. Here you will now find the sources for this evidence, here are all the overlooked inclusions, including those "twenty words", all clearly stated. No-one can honestly claim that this research is "not up to date" with "modern scholarship", for it does not rely on accepted opinions and "group-thinking" but on original research taken from the primary source itself. Modern scholarship has <u>no</u> agreed, common, evidence to offer: if you don't believe me then just look at the conflicting opinions voiced on line, there is not a shred of statistical significance to be found. Modern scholarship offers no proofs, it has been floundering for two centuries, all for lack of reading twenty words.

Of course there are readers who believe that the latest academic publication will always be the best informed, even when it displays no regard for original documents and restricts itself to repeating previously expressed opinions, that is "group-thinking" and its test of conformity with authority. My own belief has always been in scientific methodology, which is to say, in going back to the basic original and repeating the experiment from first principles. In this philosophy there is no place for "modern scholarship" and its "group-thinking", only for scientific validation.

Scientific methodology is not alien or inimical to all historical studies as some people claim, in reality it should underpin them, as it does for the whole structure of our technological world. Our English history is unique and this doubly unique ancient document is of world importance. We are now in the 21st century and we must leave the past behind if we are to comprehend our history. Our past must now be "evidence based" if it is not to be a fairy-story, if it is not to be "false news"! Science, not faith, is what we require.

Well, that is one approach but should we instead look to the anti-scientific fairy-stories of history, should we instead embrace the comfort of "group-thinking"? It saves us the effort of thinking and reinforces faith. Censorship is a valid proposition because it is designed to bring comfort and to avoid dispute. Read the evidence presented here and then make up your own mind, make a decision for either truth or comfort, these are the alternatives on offer.

CHAPTER TWO

Academic Night-Hawking: Where is the Tomb?

We all like to think we know our history but all too often history is concerned with spectres, ghosts of the past, people we cannot actually see: it is insubstantial and lacks proper definition. Historians love to advance new theories, new ghosts and wraiths, that is their business, but so often there is nothing that you can actually seize hold of, in order to prove to yourself what they are saying. History is something you are told to believe, though you can never see or touch its reality, and then you are told to unbelieve in order to accept something else that has now come along in its place. This is "modern scholarship", yet those who quote near-contemporary testimonies and chronicles may themselves only be repeating ancient inventions and these things are impossible to prove either way. Just how can we find the truth?

The further back you look in time the worse the focus becomes, the poorer are the optical aids (you might say) and so the greater is the faith required. People and places and what those people did in those places, that is what you really want to know if you believe in the value of history, you also require the evidence that will sort facts from romantic fiction. It is tantalising to be told something new and we want to believe what we are told, but how do we <u>prove</u> it? Being rational and scientific in our modern world, not being perhaps as strongly religious as our forefathers were, we are inclined to ask for proof in order to validate the proffered "facts". We no-longer accept faith alone, but how can we trust "proof" that has no evidential foundation?

Just suppose you had a time-machine and could then go back 900 or 1,000 years, would that provide proof? Suppose you could return and see ancient English landscapes, and in them the occupations of our ancestors; suppose that in spite of being unable to interrogate these ancestors you could, nevertheless, read some of their thoughts, look into their minds, watch their actions. What then, what if? That would be real history would it not, better than stories accepted on faith. Wouldn't that be like stepping onto another planet, a trip in space and time? You would be exploring what no-one else had seen in 900 years, no, not a living soul.

Arguably England's greatest national treasure, maybe even her very greatest national achievement, goes by an obscure name and is shrouded in mystery. It is called "Domesday Book". Domesday Book, is a massive document of maybe two million words, not only unique in its age but also for centuries to come, a creation and a mechanism centuries ahead of its time. It is packed with statistics, with facts, yet it remains an enigma. In fact it has remained Enigma-coded to many generations of scholars; it is a "closed book" to those who study its encrypted folios, folios which simultaneously excite and frustrate both historians and students of history alike.

Domesday Book is a time-machine well over 900 years old whose mechanisms have only (so far) been explained by speculations and by wild and even opposing theories. Its potential is obvious but its reality is inaccessible. It is a mechanism from the past which cannot be made to work, cannot be set in motion and so its scientific validation cannot be proven, or so it is maintained, so it is thought, yet clearly it once functioned. Once upon a time the few who were allowed to read it knew what it said. They knew its real importance.

In spite of hundreds of books and learned articles no scholar can tell you how to read it, how to decode what it says, what the statistics mean, whatever these scholars might claim. It remains no more than a translation, one of unfathomed content and meaning. Though it is so obviously important yet it is maddeningly frustrating. If the men who wrote and compiled it almost one thousand years ago (and parts of its information might be even older), if <u>they</u> knew its purpose and could read its contents, why can we not do the same? Were they cleverer than us, or was it all a vast mistake and folly? Was it a waste of time and effort? Surely not! Just consider the time and the effort expended and ask yourself if we could do the same today given only horse and foot transport, only pen, ink and parchment (or vellum) by which to record so much information, covering thirty-four counties in perhaps six months. The test of its greatness is that no-one else ever managed to replicate it (or anything like it), to do it again and, I suggest, that is the test of its potential. That is its validation.

"The text of Domesday Book is notoriously ambiguous, its array of social and economic statistics hitherto inaccessible", according to the Hull Project, which has compiled an on-line translation but has still not provided any demonstrable reconciliation of this data – because the "book" could not be read, it was still only a translation when they began. Even computers need facts, statistics and parameters, to work on, translations alone are inadequate. One day "artificial intelligence" will replace the human brain and group thinking, but until then, the machines need data.

Yes, I said it could not be read, but that is until now, for now I am going to show you <u>how</u> to read it. I am going to tell you what that twenty-word "key" says and where to find it, what the units mean and meant and <u>how to prove them</u>, I am going to show you the arithmetic which sets this ancient mechanism running once again. I am going to show you how to set it out in order to read it like any modern survey and when you have this secret at your fingertips you will be able to see those ancestors of one thousand years ago. You will be able to see people and places that have long disappeared, see them for the first time, see what others have not seen, see them in three-dimensions and in colour. You will be a time-traveller and a discoverer.

As I promised, you will even have the means to discover their mental processes and consequently you will understand our ancestors as never before. You will see history revealed and in the flesh. The shadows in the crypt beckon and they say, "open, read and I'll come to thee".

"For nothing that happened in the past is dead to the man
who would know how the present came to be what it is"

CHAPTER THREE

Measuring the Grave: The Problem of Lengths

In point of fact we are not "night-hawking" for it is context that turns treasure into history and the recovery of the context is our purpose. The key to all probative scientific knowledge lies in the use of statistics, and statistics are not lies but are <u>proven</u> facts and figures. The key to their proof is a combination of logic and arithmetic and these tools are very different from being dependant on the "mention of dead authorities". Instead they depend on "Occam's Razor", the scientific principle of going back to basics and starting the experiment again. First prove that it either works or doesn't work but don't accept someone else's word on trust. Don't twist the evidence in order to "prove" a theory. The opinions and speculations of others need to be validated for only religion is a matter of blind belief.

So let us start again, let us make our start by reviewing the statistical expressions employed 900 years ago in order to see if we can retrieve units, units apparently set-down in such profusion and with such diligence by the clerks involved in compiling Domesday Book. These things are the keys to the society we seek and we need to test them to see if they embody constant values, for we have so often been told that they are no more than nonsense. We also need to know what the expressions employed meant then, at that time, for what an expression means now may not be the same at all.

First of all we will look at units of length, the league, the mile, the furlong and sometimes the perch and the acre. Just occasionally we encounter feet. For some of us the mile is not so strange, when we were at school it was 1,760 yards, but yards are not units we encounter in Domesday Book, neither are miles. Many authorities have claimed that it was impossible for our ancestors to maintain what is called a "statute mile" and that we can apply this principle to any ancient unit. Nothing, so they have said, is consistent. Well, if this was so, why in 1086 did they make use of words that had no definitions in order to express units devoid of values?

Maybe miles were not so often employed because they did not think in large numbers of yards? Maybe it was easier to add up smaller units than a mile, units one can see? There are eight furlongs (of 220 yards) in a mile and we encounter furlongs all the time. However, multiplication by eights is not a simple task, in the absence of times-tables. The practised eye can estimate a furlong pretty quickly but a string of them is not so easy to see when the ground goes up and down. If they could not define a furlong they could not define an acre (of 22 x 220 yards) for the furlong, or "shot", is its long side, yet acres occur all the time, so they <u>could</u> do that. After all, our ancestors could define and maintain coin purities (alloys) and their (minute) grain weights quite precisely, we know that from analysing their pennies.

Of course there are distinguished modern academics who maintain that the furlong was not a unit at all, in spite of Domesday Book's consistent employment of it as such, but instead an infinitely variable length designed to walk a plough without the need to turn it. Well, quite apart from the efficacy of ploughing in opposite directions, just how far could the poor oxen be made to heave before they fell down dead! Even oxen need a breather and 220 yards would be a sensible point to choose, besides even a wheeled plough is not that heavy. Maybe a "long furlong" expression was employed in a generalised way, much as we might say "just ten minutes by road", but the furlong quite clearly had a specific unitary value for practical people using unitary formulae in 1066-1086.

Let us assume that they were as clever as us, not inferior to us, and then we will soon be able to establish whether they were accurate or not in measuring lengths. They weren't cleverer than us, they just did things in different ways. Already we have managed a glimpse into their world.

CHAPTER FOUR

Validation: Whose is the Body?

This is simple: in any equation the arithmetic will not work if we get even one value, one statistic or unit, wrong. One error and the whole thing will fail when we come to validate it against a demonstrable standard. Stay with me and you will see that our arithmetic does not fail and that it can be validated, because if we finally do have a correct set of units, we will be able to check ancient areas against much more recent surveys. That will begin to provide some basic context for our treasure and that will also provide our proof. Up to now all such attempts have failed.

So, let us give some consideration to the problem of lengths and distances, which so many historians have found to be a challenge. For some reason, though these Domesday Surveys did not use the mile unit, they found the league unit very attractive. That was the way they thought. What distance was a league? Some scholars have claimed it was a distance of one-and-a-half miles. I don't know why they decided on this and their arithmetic has always failed. According to one scholar no amount of arithmetical ingenuity will reconcile the Domesday entries. Well, take it from me that two-and-a-half miles to a league works, that is 4,400 yards or 20 furlongs. Perhaps it was easier to divide a series of furlongs by half and then by ten rather than by the eight required for a mile? Remember, their arithmetic was cast on a chequer-board, they did not have Arabic numerals, or they counted on their fingers, all ten of them.

The perch (later embellished as the rod, pole or perch) seems to have been, "semper", then as now, 16½ feet. An odd fraction but 40 perches make a furlong – and the furlong is the long side of a visualised acre. Modern authors have devised both "long" and "short" (regional) perches, respectively 18 feet and 15 feet in length. The argument for a 15 foot perch in the layout of small and built-sites seems convincing enough but the use of a median, 16½ feet (English), does lend itself satisfactorily as an aliquot of the defined (220 yards) furlong and Domesday Book leaves us in no doubt that both units were used for precise measurements in 1086. Of course there is a world of difference between laying-out a building or a development site, on the one hand, and estimating the measurements of entire landscapes or even landscape features on the other, they lie in different worlds. The foot, rarely encountered in Domesday, was 12 inches and like the three-foot yard, not so easy to cast with counters on a chequer-table or on your fingers, but such small units are rarely required in the larger scheme of landscapes. We must learn to think like peasantry rather than as products of a modern, universal education.

Strange as it may seem we will find that our basic units of linear measurement were accurately maintained across 34 shires even though, as we shall see, area (areal) units, units conveying square measure, did (simultaneously) include three different systems. These Domesday Surveys were partly compiled from existing records, certainly the areal units were, though the linear units in particular seem to have been deponed (testified) by formal juries composed of local peasants. These linear units seem to be infilling the earlier and known records in many (but not all) cases, in which case their values were certainly "universally" known or this would not have been possible.

Sometimes these juries were from a vill (village), sometimes from a hundred or wapentake (sub-division of a shire), sometimes from the shire, so pretty-well everyone in a given locale had to know what they were talking about. Add to this the fact that their major land-owners (land-lords) generally had widely scattered estates and so did not want to find that units in one place were significantly different to another! Modern historians have, indeed, endorsed such standardised distribution by claiming that prestige and "town planning", using a 15 foot perch, links widely dispersed royal and ecclesiastical sites. It seems an inescapable conclusion that unitary values were fixed and precise.

CHAPTER FIVE

Who Made These Records?

That said, we will see with our areal values that some units were known only in England. We can forget that old "canard" that monks and priests measured everything on the spot (an impossibility), these surveys were accomplished in about six months, so even if the basic working structure was "on record" already, the extra (local) details required by the King (and these were many) were a task in themselves. As "extras" they were deponed locally, by peasant jurymen on oath. Moreover, the clerks who wrote it all down had to be fluent in the local language (English of some sort, varying with the district), in Latin (in which it was set-down) and in French (of some sort) as spoken by most landholders and by the King's commissioners, who were there to represent royal authority but many of whom could neither read nor write, certainly not count, for such things did not concern them. Measuring every acre, at every vill, 13,418 places, all in the space of six months, was, of course, impossible, a ridiculous suggestion for any scholar to make, just as silly as supposing that French monks would be fluent in three languages and versed in units unique to England!

This is, perhaps, the most important point, both the "hide" and the "sulung" are not found as either nouns or units anywhere else in Europe or Scandinavia. Whilst foreign scholars may have known of Cassiodorus' work and apparently employed 15 foot (perch) squares in order to layout perfect rectilinear plans and enceintes for ecclesiastical and royal enclosures, which certainly would have impressed a layman with their perfect right angles, they did not survey the English countryside in a 15 foot grid pattern and then deposit permanent records which somehow survived, somewhere, for hundreds of years. Neither could they have measured 34 shires in approximately six months in 1086. Thousands of Domesday entries testify that the hide was purely English and so a mystery to foreigners.

Of course, the fact that some units were purely English, not Norman, Breton or French, meant that the clerks certainly could not have been monks and priests from outside England who would have measured in lieue, toise and arpent. No, these clerks were special and could understand English units, they were specially trained royal household clerks, the men one scholar identified as CAMERARII and, being so, they were not open to any threats or bribes from the rich and powerful. This was a breed apart, a special breed of royal servants who owed their very safety to their loyalty to their royal master. He protected them from abuse by the rich and the powerful and their lives depended on their probity.

CHAPTER SIX

Autopsy: What Do the Linear Units Record?

Right, we can now say that we have a relatively simple set of linear units to hand and that these units were generally employed across England in order to calculate areas of specific land-use, land-uses not always set down in any earlier documents (unless, perhaps in land-grants and charters) but instead largely local assessments used by the local peasantry. Such specific uses were quite separate from the broad assessments of area which we will discuss in due course. We will discuss all these in due course. Now and for the first time nation-wide records were being made of purely local features and uses and it is here that our language difficulties arise, not in translation but in local meanings.

Think about it, when do trees become a wood, when is a fallow or lea-sow a set-aside? Where do land uses interface? The King now wanted (in particular) to know about "woodlands" and "meadows" and "pastures" everywhere, in every place, but what did these nouns mean to the men of 34 highly individual shires who heard them and who farmed such lands? Not surprisingly, we find all sorts of other details creeping in. Puzzled peasants, fearful of royal authority, tried to answer honestly – so, when asked what size a field was, or what type of land it was, they sometimes replied, "I don't know, but (in season) it is very fruity ground". How big was a copse, "I don't really know, very small, just a little underwood". And the clerks set it all down just as it came, that was their training. Even monks did the same in the scriptorium, their job was to set things down in writing, such clerks had no editorial or executive powers. They were there to translate and to write down verbatim, that was a clerk's training. The lords "commissioners" (LEGATI) provided the royal authority, but they had neither knowledge of nor interest in "peasant matters" and could not give advice. This was an exercise in records collection but the <u>precise</u> meaning of the common nouns employed was subject to local appreciation (as is often the case today!). In 1086 there was no such thing as a lexicon or a dictionary of definitions and there was no universal education.

The people who had always known the land and how to use it were the peasantry and they had to know what each other worked and what it measured. It was men among them, reeves, who kept the records because their masters had no interest in agriculture and most could neither read, write nor count. Localities were local knowledge as there were no maps so land holders, lords, needed the testimony of peasants when any area or estate had to be described. We see this in surviving charters where "bounds" are given in local and natural landscape features.

CHAPTER SEVEN

Why Both Linear and Areal Units?

Quite simply, purely local things that had not been measured and set-down before now had to be expressed in units, for these "outsiders", and the easiest solution was to say what the length and breadth might be or, if small, how many acres. The calculation of very large areas must have taken some time, piecing bits together, like a jigsaw. Precisely defined and already recorded land-uses were easier to express in areal units: how many (arable) ploughlands, well that area was already known. How large was an area for tax-purposes, that was already in the geld records and we will come to them in due course. How many ploughs were at work now on the arable? That was easy to answer. How large are your pastures, well that depends on what you mean by "pastures"? Specific, non-arable, landscapes could be a problem.

So there were woods, moors, wastes, pastures, lea-sows, fens, marshes, meadowlands, fisheries, mills and so-on, all requiring reduction (if possible), as the King had ordered, to "woodlands", "meadows" and "pastures". In addition he wanted to know how much arable land had there been in 1066 (using the ploughs at work then as units) and how much land/how many ploughs, there now? Why was this information necessary, because the King wanted to know "if more can be had". That was an important part of his instructions, we have his brief on record. This was England's (and Europe's) first tax-audit and one comparing records and assets. Records do not remain constant, land uses change over time, 1086 was not 1066, so the records were to be updated.

So let us start with these local depositions by men who couldn't read or write but <u>could</u> count, peasants testifying to royal commissioners (legati), chief lords who were largely illiterate and innumerate, and who could not understand their language, but whose clerks (camerarii) were indeed omnicompetent, though without the authority of the noble commissioners in the peasant's eyes. Commissioners represented the king, the clerks made the records, but if they had had to measure everything they would never have finished the task. The new measurements were given by the peasantry, sitting empanelled in juries.

"The length of these units is open to doubt..."[1]... "the significance of this type of entry is obscure... nor can we hope to convert these measurements into modern acreages by some arithmetical process"[2], or so we have been told. Well, someone had already measured everything in broad terms and only locals knew the finer details. These new surveys would put the two blocks of information together.

We have been trained to believe that the English peasantry were as ignorant as their new foreign landholders; we have been told to believe in the total inferiority of the inferior social classes, but these peasants knew what they meant, what one-another meant, and how things worked, and so did the royal clerks. Quite apart from "local knowledge", someone had to know how agriculture worked if everyone was to eat! It certainly wasn't the lords, temporal or spiritual. They were only interested in what their bond-tenants produced for them.

The contention of this study is that the units of Domesday Book <u>can</u> be converted to acres by consistently applying arithmetical process and that the results <u>can</u> be validated by reference to more recent surveys because units, if not the precise definitions of nouns, were consistent. The peasantry had already measured-up their workaday world in workaday units, they could not otherwise have cultivated, or maintained cultivation of, the land. The validation for this is not restricted to a handful or even to a hundred reconciliations, it relies on thousands of satisfactory statistical results which can now be recovered from the Domesday Surveys. Yes, the validation lies in many <u>thousands</u> of reconciliations!

CHAPTER EIGHT

Measuring the Bones: The Linear Units

No doubt it seems arrogant to claim that reconciliation between linear units and acres is possible when so many others have failed to achieve any semblance of consistency. However, remember what I said about first principles and the need to start again from basics? At the root of these first principles lies language. Here is our disconnect, what did a given word mean? Just as a disarticulated skeleton is difficult to estimate in height, because of the interposition of epiphyses in a living body, so we must look for the connecting tissues of language and attempt to estimate "ossification". The real problem is not in measuring lengths but in the exact contemporary meanings of words.

We need to understand their language in 1066-1086, by which I do not mean the translation (which we certainly have) but, instead, the contemporary import, or use, of each noun at each location. To do this we need to understand their society and, in particular, their lack of formal education, for everything we are going to examine will, essentially, be self-taught and pragmatic. However, I think we can be reasonably confident that the recording (royal) clerks were quite competent to translate from Old English to the Latin in which their (shorthand) record was made. Fortunately they were not required to define terms, their business was to set down whatever was said, they were recording machines not lexicons or school-masters. If someone said "this is pasture", that is what the clerks set down. Whether that noun had exactly the same meaning in every locality is another matter – and remains so even to today.

This was a world of small social units, sometimes isolated groups but mostly cohesive, often as a collection of small communities, often as administrative or judicial units called "hundreds" or "wapentakes", divisions of a shire, though sometimes men also met in their own shire court. These then were the social units where men did business, one with another, where they met to exchange goods and services, to grant land and assets, to hear the law and to witness. Within given areas, or groups of men, they had to understand, everyday, what they were each saying, one to another, though today, thanks to formal education, we have forgotten this. Lexicons and further education have taught us to think broadly alike and not to think for ourselves. Sometimes this helps, sometimes we are, still and nevertheless, mistaken.

These men were, therefore, independent thinkers and the members of each group had to know exactly what their neighbours meant. Today we think we know what we are saying – at least until we get to court and are forced to be more precise – but these men <u>knew</u> what their immediate neighbours meant. They did not necessarily know, however, what men in the next county meant when they employed the same noun. The suspicion surely is that we are often looking at ancient political divisions, at ancient kingdoms now forgotten but each of whom once did things "their way".

CHAPTER NINE

Back to Basics: General Physiology

Skeletons do exhibit features in common, albethey of many different formations and occurrence. What our "dead authorities" forgot when they tried to solve this problem of measurement is that whilst unitary values can be fixed as constants, everyday usage of language is much less precise. The trained anatomist may speak in a very different vocabulary to the layman, such as "external auditory meatus" or "gonial angle", but this is the result of training. Without it we use our own terms. We should not expect more of our 1066 English peasants than we do of ourselves!

The nouns to which these linear units of Domesday Book were attached were not even defined by their Old English language, by law or by lexicons, to unequivocal meanings, so men did their best to comply with the King's demands and this meant that they applied the meaning which that word had for them in their local group. Even today we do not use words like "pasture" and "woodland" with anything like absolute precision; vernacular comprehension of such land-uses is quite imprecise[3] and even legal definition is still open to debate.[4] Back then, however, in each area where a definition was locally understood, men expressed themselves with a cogency not comprehended today and a lucidity not required by modern education. Of course, the Church had knowledge of obscure and esoteric things but it was the peasantry who received an education in the things that really mattered, like how to farm and grow food.

Thus the basic requirement of subsistence farmers was always arable land, ploughed land, so the best soils available were used to grow wheat, barley and oats and their extents (areas or sizes) were a matter of local record. Any changes in such local pictures (between 1066 and 1086) would be picked-up when the plough totals, the ploughs actually at work in 1086, were stated by local juries. But the King wanted to know three other land-uses as well, uses maybe not recorded in writing before this, and he wanted them for every place.

The beauty of this official formula was that in every place all three <u>would</u> be found – meadow, woodland and pasture – because (in some form) they occur everywhere, so that if one of them was not separately identified, locally, it was obviously subsumed in one of the others and what mattered to the Crown was not the application of a text-book definition to the landscape but a count of the overall areas of land involved. The purpose behind asking these basic questions was to build-up an audit picture of a total landscape. Why, well we will come to that in due course.

CHAPTER TEN

Woodlands

Let us start with "woodlands", everyone will think that an easy definition. Not so! Even today we do not use this classification with anything like precision, probably because we have forgotten the real value of woodlands. To the majority of the medieval peasantry, who were subsistence farming, the most relevant use of "wood" was as "firibusque" (to borrow a medieval aphorism), the firewood essential for the baking of "breadibus". Yet "wood" is not the same as "woodland". Of course, underwood and timber do have other important uses, such as "housebot", "ploughbot", "hedgebot", but these were less important than fuel. We also need to know that in such wood-dependant societies fuel is rarely derived from arboreal denudation of the landscape, even if the necessary technology for heavy timber conversion is available (and it was not). No, fuel had to be from a renewable resource and not from timber.

Timber (proper) and wood (proper) can be quite different from domestic wood-fuel, which is <u>anything</u> that might burn, peat, ling, furze, loppings, so that a mixed landscape of underwood and secondary woodland, common and moorland, might <u>all</u> be understood as "woodland". How many oaks were needed for a woodland, maybe (in places) none at all in this sense. Neither "wood" nor (for that matter) "forest" need include large trees. "Forest" is a legal and jurisdictional term, it need not involve tree-cover at all. Then again, there might be places which grouped all rough-pastures and commons together as "pasture" even though it included secondary woodland. At times local definitions would interface but that didn't matter to the Domesday clerks. Their business was not to classify, so they did their duty and set down what was said.

So, when addressing the problem of Domesday linear measurements some scholars have declared that the difficulty is in finding a common yardstick[5] and in a way (not the way they meant, I think) they were right. A yardstick is a physical measure and the clerks were not measuring, neither were they using yards. But such scholars had made a serious misjudgement, which is this. By ignoring the heterogeneity of English (1066) society and seeking instead to impose some modern homogeneity, scholars excluded themselves from any consideration of social influences. For not only would the definitions of nouns vary from shire to shire, the arrival of incomers, new arrivals in a given locality, might then import otherwise alien unitary values. This becomes most obvious when, just here and there, new "French" tenants measured their meadows in the "arpents" otherwise reserved (in Domesday Book) for viticulture, instead of in the time-honoured local "acres".[6] This is one reason why some woodlands were measured in acres, some by length and breadth and others by swine totals. Another reason was size and another the use of a local definition of "woodland".

Thus at Rollestone in the Offlow Hundred of Staffordshire, the "wood pasture" could be and was being ploughed by 1086. Obviously not all of it was treescape. In this shire woods and wood-pastures were generally expressed in double-linears (length x breadth) but with smaller entries (perhaps more closely defined uses) expressed in acres. In Pirehill Hundred "2", "3" and "4" acres were employed instead of furlongs, for a ½ x ½ furlong would not be precise enough (at 2½ acres).

In Cuttlestone and Totmanslow Hundreds, however, they preferred to use "1 furlong" or "2 furlongs", not acres, for small measurements, but this amounts to the same thing for a furlong is the long side of an acre. Each hundred, we might say, to its own logic.

In Nottinghamshire we read of "woodland <u>not</u> pasture" which tells us that the "wood-pastures" were generally recognised as omnibus expressions containing both. In Huntingdonshire we see pastures generally lumped under "silva pastura" with the large entries in linear units and the smaller "silvae minutae" in acres, so the latter were, often, probably real and specialised woods of some value. Robert of Rhuddlan's lands at Rhos and Rhufonoig came to 69,120 acres all told, but only 2,400 acres were arable, "for all the rest is woodland and moors and cannot be ploughed" – though not all of this was covered with trees or even ling (heather), for in (rocky) places there were falcon's eyries.

There are also many aspecific entries for small areas obviously considered (locally) to be of no real value and therefore not woodlands in the commercial sense. At Canterbury (and many other places) we have "unfruitful woodland" and in Eastry Lathe, Kent, at Wingham, Easole and Adisham "small woods for fencing", which at face-value would not be fit for agistement of livestock, or for fuel. Of course, we are relying on honesty and Kent was not then, necessarily, the best example. We shall come to honesty in time but for the majority of the peasantry the royal authority represented by the "commissioners" probably scared them witlessly honest, when not under the glare of their own landlord! That is why the crown generally made sure that local peasants sitting in such juries did not have to depone before their own landlords. The king, the Crown, wanted to hear the truth!

CHAPTER ELEVEN

Pastures

So to "pasture", an associative land-use, not even defined today in legal terms which would encompass medieval agronomic practices (such as wood-pasture) and which in 1066-1086 might mean many things. For a start, some shires did not enter "meadows" and it is clear that in these shires it was the practise to subsume meadows with the pastures; so in these the specialised, small grazings were put together with the broader grazings or maybe even woodland-pastures. Yet whatever the English peasantry in different shires meant by "pasture", of one sort or another, it is evident that they were all thinking in terms of agistment, grazings, maybe sometimes mowings, with options for lea-sows and set-aside. No doubt the king had deduced as much.

Some shires were quite vague, "pastura ad pecuniam", that is grazings sufficient for the beasts of the vill, the precious plough-beasts or oxen, because the local men did not understand how to isolate pastures from other uses such as fallows. Locally they made no such distinctions. In so many places it is evident that fallows (whether temporary or permanent) were entered as "pasture" and it is equally evident that the ability to "take-in" or "sod bust" such fallows was of interest to the 1086 surveys, being generally responsible for any increase in ploughs by 1086 ("land for ploughs"). The records of 1066 were being compared with the reality in 1086 in order to note any changes, because changes in output meant wealth generation. Plough more, reap more, someone has more.

That men tried to make distinctions between different topographies is not in question, the problem is to decide what they meant in their different groups and locations. So in Nottinghamshire "underwood" is never confused with "wood pastures", though exactly the tree-cover of the former and the agistement of the latter is problematic. They knew what they meant and we often find quantities of 10,15,20,35 acres, even up to 320 acres of "wood pastures". In Rutland at Hambleton (f.293v) "there is underwood, fertile in places(!), three leagues by one and a half leagues" – viz. 28 square miles! No wonder it was "fertile" in places and capable of being ploughed. "Sod-busting" was something these surveys were sent out to detect, but they were also noting potential.

CHAPTER TWELVE

Meadows

"Meadows" were usually entered as small units, precious little plots, so in many shires they are in acres. The majority of shires had quantities of less than 50 acres of meadows in any vill and a rather smaller group of shires had quantities of less than 100 acres in any vill. At Chilton Foliot in Wiltshire we see "two by one furlongs", or 20 acres of meadow, but at Odstock as well as some large pasture we see "in another place five acres pasture", which was surely a meadow? However, in the East Midlands, including Bedfordshire and Hertfordshire, they showed less discrimination by entering "meadows" in carucates (that is in 120 acre units), so here instead of careful management for hay crops we are looking at meadowland within pastureland.[7] So in Bedfordshire we have "meadow for the oxen" at Stanford (f.218v), indicating the "pastura ad pecuniam" entries we saw above.

When we examine the precision of some entries in some shires we can only conclude that their unitary progression was far from accidental: such organisation suggests planned meadows. Thus in the Aylesford Lathe of Kent we go down to half acres and up in a sequence of one to 16 acres, then 20 and 21, 30 to 33, 40, 43, 50 and 60 acres. If these were seasonally managed, then they would have been artificially created next to rivers, though a strange academic controversy concerns "flood meadows". As far back as Roman times there were both "wet" and "dry" meadows[8] and, as Darby observed, it is natural for meadows to be situated along water courses. Rackham, however, was adamant that "flood meadows" were a 16th century introduction.[9] I suppose it depends on the degree of managed flooding.

At Bottlebridge in Huntingdonshire, "the weir of the abbot of Thorney is doing harm to 300 acres of meadow", which sounds as if seasonal meadow-flooding was being seriously impaired. These particular meadow acres were in the joint ownership of several vills and this (in turn) helps explain some of the other, larger, meadow entries we sometimes see: such a desirable resource being managed in a sort of parage. On the other hand, where waters did not exist, nevertheless rich lenses of upland soil might have formed and created "Alpine meadows", lush and mowable pockets of land, even though not situated on water courses. Where your best grass grows (and can be mown in season), that is a meadow.

CHAPTER THIRTEEN

The East Anglian "Extents": More Than One Burial

It is always possible to find a burial or a burial marker that has been reused, to find a palimpsest. In East Anglia (and occasionally elsewhere) we encounter "extents" of whole vills expressed in linear units, length by breadth, which appear to be lifted from some even older source than 1086. Once again scholarly opinion maintains that, "no amount of arithmetical ingenuity will make any intelligible order out of this", for relationships, "seem to be an unfathomable mystery".[10] Unfortunately, it appears that no determined attempt to retrieve such intelligible order has ever been made, as they are not a mystery.

If we apply our standard formula of unitary (linear) values to the aggregation of all the 537 "extents" separately listed in Norfolk as vills we discover that ante-1086 (or even ante-1066) this shire was measured as 1,075,211 acres. This figure very nearly approaches the area of 1,302,000 acres which M.A.F.F. gave for this county in 1955 and is equally valid for the M.A.F.F. estimate of one million acres for the agricultural area of the shire! In either case such coincidence can hardly be serendipitous and it encourages us to move from the general to the particulars listed in 1086.

A group of Norfolk parishes examined by the University of

The East Anglian "Extents": More Than One Burial

East Anglia had "extents" totalling 5,008 acres and this group was more recently surveyed at 5,127 acres.[11] Their arable capacity in 1066 had been 3,420 acres and the overall total of agricultural land came to 3,863 acres (all uses) yet all they offered to the geld was a mere 1,571 acres! So by collecting all this information together the royal clerks of 1086 now had an effective audit.[12]

In the case of West Walton, on the edge of the Wash and the extreme west of the shire, the attenuated "extent" entered most closely resembles an inning (and/or maintenance) of the Old Roman Bank, for it does not stretch inland. Here the separate 1086 aggregation of plough-totals and "meadows" was recorded as 1,558 acres which we can compare to the "extent" given as 1,600 acres. Also entered were many salterns, a fishery and grazings for both sheep and swine. Clearly there was a very large salt-making industry here, which accounts for the large number of inhabitants by 1086. No doubt the grazings were marsh-feedings outside the seawall and also on the fens for what was outside the "extent" was not ploughland, curtilage or meadow, it was marginal land, seasonally inundated.

Curiously no "extents" were entered in 1086 for the surrounding, adjacent, vills of Walpole, Walsoken and the Terringtons (arguing, perhaps, for a very early date for both West Walton and her extent, something long before these other places had been reclaimed) but their vital statistics were entered in 1086, so they were there by then and we can now aggregate them along with West Walton. Altogether this total group of settlements covered at least 4,494 acres and was within the seawall by 1086, an area which White's Directory of 1836 gave as 4,480 acres, though the official total in 1840 was given as 5,516 acres and may then have included saltings beyond the Wall (called the Roman Bank).[13] It seems as though West Walton had been the original focus of marshland settlement here and that the system of "extents" was therefore a good deal older than even the geld records.

Far to the south of the shire, on the Suffolk border, Guiltcross and Shropham Hundreds returned "extents" of 30,400 acres and 37,200 acres, together 67,600 acres. In 1845 they were measured as 26,828 and 44,944 acres, a joint area of 71,772 acres.[14] Guiltcross returned only 7,024½ acres for geld in 1086, or 23% of her "extent", but actually was ploughing 44%; Shropham returned 12,538¼ acres for geld, or 33%, but was ploughing 53%! In the 19th century Guiltcross was said to be "typically in grain" at 31-32%! The value of the 1086 audit paradigm (and its inclusion of "extents") is self-evident. What we might term "the Treasury" was accumulating information of all kinds in 1086, information of importance not only for purposes of taxation but also in order to ascertain agricultural potential. In Guiltcross and Shropham they were sod-busting even better than they managed eight centuries later, but perhaps they were desperate for grain? We will look at such comparisons in a later chapter.

CHAPTER FOURTEEN

Establishing Identity: Other Anomalies and Proofs

In Nottinghamshire in Thurgarton, Newark and Lythe Wapentakes we encounter furlong and virgate mixtures. Here I take the virgate to be an expression of a linear "quarter", just as "furlong" was sometimes applied to length but sometimes to an acre's area. Rather than being the areal (square) measure of one quarter hide (we will come to areas next), therefore, the virgate would here be a length of a quarter of an acre's length, or a quarter of a "shot", viz. 55 yards. Thus "two acres by a virgate" would be 440 yards x 55 yards = five acres. Then "nine furlongs by 50 virgates" becomes 1,980 yards x 2,750 yards = 5,445,000 square yards = 1,125 acres. Similarly "eight furlongs by 14 virgates" becomes 1,760 yards (one mile) x 770 yards = 1,355,200 square yards = 280 acres. So at Kelham (f.293) we see eight furlongs by eight virgates (one mile by a quarter of a mile) = 160 acres, but also at the "other Kelham" (f.285v) "underwood" of 16 furlongs by 74 virgates = 2,960 acres. It seems a strange way of thinking but it is clearly intrinsic (local) rather than forensic (imposed) by some peripatetic scribe – a man who then, perversely, expressed himself elsewhere in other units! <u>It is the proof</u> that the Domesday clerks recorded what they heard, rather than measuring for themselves (if we needed such proof!). I wonder why no-one ever noticed this before?

I think we can also propose that these Nottinghamshire

peasants were not possessed of adding machines, at least nothing more sophisticated than fingers or a chequer-board on which to visually cast accounts, so the lengths which they deponed must have approximated in some way to the lengths and breadths which they actually saw, even if some of them sometimes employed alternative units. We will see that exactly the same anomalous arithmetic occurred when men chose square, or areal, units rather than linear ones. Remember, when we consider the values of the units employed, no-one had "times tables" so all arithmetic relied on simple aids such as fingers. Easier to count in quantities of tens than in twelves. Easier to halve and quarter than to apply fractions. Nevertheless, sometimes abacus methodology (the chequer board) permitted the addition of quantities which were expressed as large products.

CHAPTER FIFTEEN

The Grave Goods: Mineral Rights

In Cornwall we discover large tracts of "pastures" and "woodlands" measured in linear units. We will not be surprised to discover that the King laid claim to "terra regis" of 12,000 acres of "pasture" in Tybesta Hundred, just as he laid claim to the New Forest in Hampshire, but when other magnates laid claim to 12,000, 20,000 and 32,000 acres we are surprised. In Pawton (later called Pydow) Hundred the Crown claimed 48,000 acres of "pasture" and in Winnianton Hundred were two estates claiming (together) 92,000 acres! In Oxfordshire and Berkshire the royal "forests" claimed "woodlands", as did Earl Hugh for his "forest" in Lancashire.[15] In such cases we are looking at claims over trees and soil. In Cornwall we can see something else: it is not called "forest" here and we should ask why? Well, it is because these are claims over <u>and</u> under the soil, and there is proof of this.

Without becoming involved in a lengthy explanation (I have provided the evidence elsewhere), suffice it to say that in places such as these, in Cornwall, we discover patterns of intensive agricultural production ringing-round locations with high populations but (strangely) with no proper provision for subsistence. These places either have no ploughs or too few to sustain their community. Clearly, in such cases, we are looking at populations of artisans, men <u>buying</u> their sustenance from the local sources around them and in order to do this they must be in the money economy. When we observe that these artisan-hubs coincide with known (later) mining districts and also the Stanneries (first recorded after c.1200) the mystery is solved, we are looking at mineral extraction. Just over the border with Devon, at South Tawton, is confirmatory archaeological evidence of tin-streaming. Moreover, in north-west Derbyshire we see the same phenomena covering the lead-mining district.[16] Mineral rights and mineral extraction (by great lords) are the explanation, for whoever claims the soil claims what lies beneath the surface.

Yet the whole purpose of Domesday Book was to check, to audit, the land-tax, there was no provision for recording industries, so we see the clerks concerned with collecting the details quietly entering those details which evidenced other sources of wealth, presumably as part of their briefing? The man who was directing this survey/audit for the king would have been responsible for editing the surveys and, presumably, for detecting new and potential sources of taxation. Not so very long after 1086 we see such information being put to good use by the Crown's exchequer, including the creation of the stannery monopoly.

CHAPTER SIXTEEN

Summary: Ready Reckoner

I have made a compilation of many of the linear expressions (or unitary combinations) found in Domesday Book in an Appendix, which I hope will prove useful to others. I have grouped them first in furlong multiples, then in leagues with furlongs (and sometimes perches) and then a more miscellaneous group of heterogeneous units. These last particularly represent the East Anglian "extents", though I have included two from Thurgarton Wapentake in Nottinghamshire and another from outside it. These examples I believe provide the clearest possible evidence that in using such measurements men were attempting to set very accurate bounds to their vills, even if some vills subsequently sub-divided in the period between the creation of these Anglian "extents" and the creation of the records of 1066 or 1086. If the geld was itself initiated in 991, then I believe that the "extents" were records already in existence before that date. I also fail to understand how such complex and ingenious calculations could ever have been dismissed as irrelevant.

LINEAR UNITS

1 league = 2½ miles = 4,400 yards = 20 furlongs
(1 mile = 1,760 yards = 8 furlongs) – very rare

1 furlong = 220 yards = 40 perches
(viz. a precise furlong unit, not an expression)
1 perch = 16½ feet = 5½ yards
(a median between 15 and 18 feet)
1 linear acre = 220 yards = 1 furlong
1 linear virgate = 55 yards = ¼ furlong

When no techer was in Londe
Men had craft by Goddes hande.
They that had craft so He thenne
Taught forth craft to other men.
Some craft that yet comes not in place
Some man shall have by Godes grace

(Walter Mapes c.1140-1209)

CHAPTER SEVENTEEN

Exploring the Tomb: The Areal Units

Looking down into the tomb, peering and straining our eyes in the darkness, we have come to another dimension: how much does it cover, down there, how large is the floor, where does it end? Can we make a summary of the total area involved?

Now we have come to units envisaged as areas, we might say to ancient square measures. The most controversial of all of these has (in the past) been the "hide" unit, with its "virgate" aliquot, whilst the "carucate" and "bovate" have proved less contentious. There is also a unit unique to Kent, the "sulung" with its "jugum". We will come to them, but let us take one thing at a time.

Nowhere in Domesday Book do we encounter the square mile and this seems strange to us, but we need to remember that our ancestors envisaged areas in acre strips of 220 x 22 yards when they did not measure in linear units. They had no universal education to teach them to think in either abstracts or numbers, no easy numerical progression (such as is provided by Arabic numerals) and no concept of aerial overview. Their world was strictly practical, ground level, and they relied on aggregating small and visualised areas because they had no formulae or simple systems.

I am going to commence with the "hide" unit because the elucidation of this unit, nearly half a century ago, proved to be my key to unravelling the whole, complex unitary structure of Domesday Book. For more than two centuries scholars have argued about both the purpose of the hide <u>and</u> its relation to area measurement (if any) and this has left a disastrous legacy of contention based not on logic, reason, or arithmetical demonstrations but on non-rational dogma, on pseudo-religious faith: we can call it "group thinking" in modern jargon.

For a very long time many scholars argued that the hide was not an area/areal measurement at all but, in fact, a fiscal creation, a "geld unit", unit of tax liability, though no-one could explain how it was then applied without resorting to purely arbitrary imposts. They would not entertain an acre value for it and neither could they fix a de minimus specie valuation to this unit. The idea that there might have been some relationship between taxation and area seems to have been largely ignored, though I will return to this in due course.

So, if we argue that the geld was in effect an "exchequer unit" of some sort, so must be its aliquot parts, the virgates and acres we also encounter, they will all be fiscal units, in which case the whole of Domesday Book becomes an indemonstrable hypothesis, a pointless exercise. Indeed, some scholars have actually gone so far as to argue just that, which neatly avoided the need to prove anything.[17] It was, they argued, meaningless, a waste of time and King William's great folly!

Of course the strength of this fiscal argument was that it allowed the hide to become an arbitrary and hypothetical unit without fixed, measurable purpose, which also neatly ended any need to attempt arithmetical reconciliation and by the 1880's this was a very acceptable argument. Some scholars then attempted to present it as a tax, one related in some way to landholding but raised only on the peasantry (an attractive proposition to landed Victorian gentry), so that if there was any relationship with landholding, the landholder's demesnes would have been free of tax. At first J.H. Round objected to this saying, "the exemption of the DOMINIUM would be fatal to the whole system", but then he went on to say that he could not otherwise make sense of his own theories or make them reconcile with Domesday Book.[18] He therefore came round to "beneficial hidation" and to tax exemptions. If Domesday Book said "does not pay geld" that (he thought) must have meant it was exempted taxation! Of course what it really meant was "this cheat is not paying his taxes".

He therefore concluded that "DUO NON GELDANT" (etc.) must mean "are exempted from the need to pay (geld)", so he finally agreed that lands IN DOMINIO, in lordship, were exempted, which (he claimed) was why the tax on non-demesne lands (that is the peasant's tenancies) was finally increased (for we know that the rate of the geld was finally raised) from two shillings on the hide to a massive six shillings in a "conspiracy-between the Conqueror and his barons hitherto unsuspected by historians...it is of some novelty and interest". How the tiller of a minute plot of peasant land was supposed to raise such a fortune as a penny, let alone more, was never explained.

Such a revelation was entirely in accord with the prevailing popular depiction of the Norman Conquest and its brutal oppression of the "Anglo-Saxons", as they were then called. The Victorian landed gentry were still either descended from a Norman ancestor or they aspired to be so, so this revelation of scholarship was God's determining of the Victorian social order. From then on all scholars accepted "beneficial hidation" and "fiscal hides" and perhaps some tenuous connection to area, though not necessarily a fixed area. The fact that the six shillings geld coincided with the most serious threat of invasion in the twenty years of King William's reign went entirely unnoticed![19] They seem to have had no idea that taxation might need to be spent on defence of the realm and no-one remarked that King William had been holding-off invasions from every direction for all this time.

CHAPTER EIGHTEEN

Controversy: Who Buried the Corpse?

This view of the Conquest and Round's ideas on beneficial hidation ("conspiracy") went substantially unchallenged for almost a century until Professor Galbraith's suggestion that Domesday Book was not solely a geld record. This, therefore, made the proposal of an hypothetical geld unit untenable, but without substituting an alternative purpose or conceptual unitary value.[20] So, there must be some sort of relationship with land.

Of course there are very many entries in Domesday Book which should have raised questions about Round's thinking long before this. For example, at Norbury and Wirksworth, in Cheshire, we are told that four hides do pay geld, but how could they do that if they had always been fiscally exempted? How could they be hidated? At Goostrey we are told that three virgates could be gelded (though formerly WASTA), so were those virgates not land? Were they some form of accountant's error? Peover and Tetton say the same and at Sutton we are told that acres also gelded. How then could this gelding have happened without changing the name to hides if the fiscal unit was "the hide"? How could physical acres be gelded if they were materially different to fiscal hides?

Darby and Terrett went so far as to argue that hides, carucates and ploughlands all had the same areal value, 120 acres, which (though a sensible reconciliation) inevitably led them to say that they could not comprehend the relationship between these three units, for the ploughlands and carucates for each vill in Northamptonshire did not exactly match, and this in turn led them to conclude the artificiality of everything![21] This would seem to really return us to "King William's great folly", an awkward admission for scholars engaged in the geographical relevance of the Domesday statistics. Should we conclude that the dead body <u>never</u> had substance, that it had always been a wraith!

By now it was essential to end the circular arguments and confusion, especially with the looming nonacentenary of Domesday in 1986, even if no certain relationships or values could be proven. In his superb (Phillimore) re-issue of Farley's text, with concurrent translations, Professor John Morris made the final confirmation that the hide was (perhaps) 120 acres.[22] This at last put an end to speculations which had suggested anything from 40 to 120 acres or more, yet as late as 1968 one researcher observed that as the Burghal Hidage gave Dorset 2,360 hides while Domesday gave it 2,349 hides and the Geld Rolls gave only 1,394 hides (theoretical) or 1,407 (actual), there was obviously a case for beneficial hidation! In fact with £40 still owing the Geld Rolls should have added another 133½ hides.[23]

It never seems to have occurred to anyone that taxes are often evaded and so auditing is ultimately essential. So, in spite of such seeming unanimity for a 120 acre hide the fact remained that there was no arithmetical proof, no contemporary evidence let alone any reconciliation with known and proven values, leaving Domesday Book still unread (though not untranslated) because its most important unit, the hide, could not be reconciled – and neither could virgate, carucate or ploughland! Even the size of an acre was in doubt.

In the acid soil, the corpse had dissolved to nothing more than a stain on the sand! So, we can say, it was certainly not a wraith, for wraiths have no substance to decay and a stain meant that there had once been a solid body. Where to now?

CHAPTER NINETEEN

The Solutions and Proofs: Waking the Dead

In fact the answer to this conundrum, this mensural encryption, had always been there, it was written large in Domesday Book and it was also elsewhere. Too much emphasis on academic conformity had obscured what had always been (though well hidden) in plain sight. The senior clerk, or "mandarin", the man who edited and finally compiled Domesday Book, was astute enough to leave a marker or "footnote" for posterity to find, so that his successors could verify the process involved. Deep in the text he had laid a plain statement of fact.

At Stradlie, in the Golden Valley of Herefordshire, 112 ploughs, so it was entered in 1086, could plough this place and interlined above this entry was "56 hides". The entry therefore reads, "(L VI.hidis) poteraN arare.C.& XII.carvcae". Just nine words to provide the first part of our "key", the others follow later with the companion unit. So, it is very simple: 112 ploughs could/can plough 56 hides.

At Suddington in Leicestershire the King held as, "one hide less one carucate", and the obvious conclusion would be, two carucates to one hide. At Castle Camps in the Childerford Hundred of Cambridgeshire[24] Domesday Book says "Norman holds of Aubrey half a hide, land for one plough" and of the same holding the Inquisitio Comitatus Cantabrigiensis says, "half a hide Norman holds of Aubrey, which is land for one plough". Interestingly the final total of all units in each of these two accounts, when converted to acres, is identical: 2,800 acres in each. Moreover, in 1885 the Parish of Castle Camps comprised 2,700 acres. We certainly have a working hypothesis, one verifiable not only "then" but also "now"! The plough and its carucate unit being well known as 120 acres, the hide was then 240 acres.

At Colchester in Essex, just outside the town (in 1086), the Bishop of London held two hides, one acre and six and a half acres of meadow in 1086: as we can now say, 487½ acres. In 1900 the Bishop of London held St. Mary-at-the-Walls as 487½ acres.[25] In 1903 Round himself confirmed this to be the Domesday estate and Morris' Phillimore volume endorsed this identification.

Many shires have such evidence to offer. So, if Shoyswell Hundred in the Rape of Hastings was "never gelded", then how could it be entered in Domesday Book as hidated by some supposedly fiscal unit? The hide had to be (ergo) an areal unit and not a fiscal one! At Okeford Fitzpaine in Dorset we discover "8 hides, land for 16 ploughs". In Wales we find places that were "never hidated or gelded", an unnecessary repetition if the hide was a fiscal unit but quite understandable if land had been captured and now needed taxing. The Abingdon Chronicle tells us that the hide was 240 acres, the Liber Eliensis includes several 240 acre hides and the Battle Abbey Cartulary makes similar reference.

Looking at the Giddings in Huntingdonshire Beresford and St Joseph[26] noted that in 1279 some 138 households cultivated or had fallow 3,620 acres (excluding curtilages) and that the modern area was 3,854 acres (all told). They thought the coincidence remarkable. What they did not know was that the 17½ hides of 1086, which they had also noted, were equivalent to 4,200 acres. Villages and parishes will shift their boundaries over the centuries but, unless there is some dramatic change, they will generally remain conformable.

CHAPTER TWENTY

Reconciliation: Combining the Evidence

We have now solved <u>two</u> subordinate problems at the same time as discovering the value of the hide unit. The first, why do we so often discover more carucates recorded than there are/were hides? No, the answer was never "beneficial hidation", it is simply a ratio of two to one. Second, we can see that there was a relationship between the geld (tax) and the area involved, so it was a land tax. What I believe happened to obscure this relationship was that after 1086 the hide unit came to be an Exchequer secret, for it was also a unique English unit, <u>not</u> one either known or accounted elsewhere in Europe. As landlords were not interested in agriculture so no-one outside the English peasantry would have used it by 1086.

How it was that both Church and nobility came to be in the dark is simple, they had no interest in agronomics nor in peasantries, not at this date anyway. Even if some landholders discovered the secret it was soon forgotten because, thanks to the comprehensive scope of Domesday Book, other more efficient taxes evolved to replace this land-only tax, this geld, in the next century. So, those who wrote the histories forgot, if they ever knew, the meaning and value of the humble hide and as for the Exchequer, as it ceased to make use of Domesday Book for tax purposes it also forgot the unit, let alone its well camouflaged "marker" in the Golden Valley.

The carucate, the land for a plough, was however, "universally" known and understood in 1066-1086. At Chepstow (f.162) Ralph Linsey held 50 carucates of land, "sic fit Normannia" (as is done in Normandy). The carucate, based on the eight-ox caruca (plough) was an area that could be ploughed in a year, so the number of ploughs at work in 1066 and in 1086 should tally and if it did not, one needed to look for an explanation. At Oakington in Cambridgeshire there was, "land for one and a half ploughs, there are six oxen (here) and there can be one plough (more)". The "ploughlands" were the established and recorded arable lands of an estate, whilst the ploughs at work stated the 1086 reality. If anyone had been "sodbusting", in order to make more profit, the ploughs gave them away. If they tried to hide their industry, they automatically came under suspicion and tax-evasion was treason.

Thus the hide has been the key to the whole encryption of the Domesday records. It preceded Domesday Book by several centuries and where it came from no-one knows, but it was unique to England. Originally it measured whole landscapes, as indeed it still did in some shires in 1066-1086, but by 1066 a large part of the former Danelaw, an area of England heavily populated with Danish incomers, was using the carucate instead and so only measuring arable land in the main. (See map 1). When in 991 the payment of a ransom ("danegeld") was equitably linked to landholding (in hides) a land-tax was created and from then on tax evasion was possible and desirable, from the landholder's point of view. That is why some shires did not enter hides, their occupants only understood carucates, but what a godsend that could be to the hidated shires, if one could get away with it, get away with claiming carucates not hides. It would be a serious risk, but before 1086 there were no audits, so tax evasion was possible and very tempting.

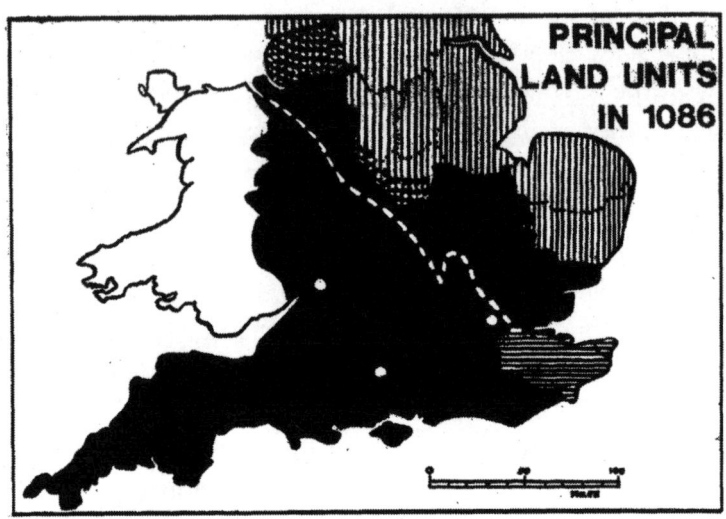

 The old border between England and the Danelaw

Shires employing hide units to measure areas

Shires employing carucate units alone

Shires combining hide and carucate units of land measurement

Kent, which employed sulung units

The three locations are London, Winchester and Gloucester

Principal Land Units in 1086

CHAPTER TWENTY-ONE

Subsequent Use of the Hide Unit: Voices of the Dead

The DIALOGUS DE SCACCARIO (c.1170), an enchiridion (guidebook) written for Henry II, written in order to explain the machinery of state, was at pains to set-down the fact that the hide is an areal unit. After that it fudges this units' value by saying that "in its primitive form" it had contained one hundred acres but, "ruricole melius hoc norunt" (country folk know, or can tell us, better, or country folk witness such things accurately)![27] So, as this book was also a highly restricted (royal) document, if any unauthorised person gained access to it and was to try to make use of this piece of secret information, their false calculations would immediately expose them as thieves. That is why I suggest that the area of the hide was, or had become by c.1170, an administrative and state secret: after all, it was the means of seeing into men's souls! Otherwise there would have been no point in hiding the real value of the hide unit. Indeed, it seems that from the outset, from the brief given in 1085, the hide's potential as an audit-tool had been recognised, magic to lay bare the secret machinations of men!

This Exchequer document then goes on to say (ablative voice) "with respect, surely in such cases it is not by earlier examples, but by reason (reckoning)", so that, "as it sometimes arises, the causes of things and the reasons of sayings <u>are</u> <u>secret</u> and then it suffices to bring forward examples relating to them, especially if they are taken from the cases (cited by) prudent men whose actions are circumspect and not done without reason… we have called nothing 'certain' unless it is what the King decreed to be observed" – le roy le vult! This certainly suggests that when the King so wished, secret calculations could be made by certain royal servants and, I believe, that this passage refers to the use of the Domesday statistics for secret and audit purposes even as late as a century after they were made. For as long as Domesday Book <u>could</u> be read it remained the ultimate survey, from which there was no appeal, for only the Crown knew what it was really disclosing.

This particular passage also seems to be of especial relevance to the separation of what we call the "greater" and the "lesser" Domesdays, which is the separation of the thirty-four folios into one gathering or collection of thirty-one and into another of only three folios. We will return to this in due course, remembering what this passage has said, for this separation has long puzzled scholars and historians.

Before we do examine the "greater" and "lesser" Domesdays we also need to know that the hide was not the only unique unit within the Domesday folios. For several reasons, including this other unique unit, Kent is very important among all the surveys and especially as she contributes our other eleven words to the solution of the mensural encryption.

CHAPTER TWENTY-TWO

Another Palimpsest: The Individuality of Kent

For some reason, lost in the Anglo-Saxon Kingdoms, by 1066 Kent had a purely individual major unit of area, the "sulung", together with its "jugum" aliquot. These were not only unique English units <u>they were units and nouns unique to Kent</u>. As with the hide unit, there have been wide-ranging scholarly discussions as to the unitary value of this noun encountered in Domesday Book (and elsewhere) and values from 100 to 200 acres have been proposed. If we look at earlier documents and in Bede's history[28] we find Thanet (and part of the mainland) anciently measured in hides and the Tribal Hidage also mentions hides, so we have a suspicion that "sulung" is the purely local name for the hide unit, one which slipped into the Domesday survey's verbatim depositions of evidence. Otherwise, why was it not evidenced before 1086? Let us once again look for clues within the text of our helpful muniment.

Sure enough, when we examine "The Possessions of Saint Martin's", "the community of St Martin's", Scortesbroc, we find, yet again, that there is no need for guess-work, for the entry reads, "funt.cccc^{te}.acres.& dimid.qae sunt. II.solinos & dimid." – there are 400 acres (of land) and a half, which is two sulungs and a half"; very simple, 400+200 acres = 600 acres which is 2x240+120=600 acres. Sulung and hide were identical and so the "jugum" aliquot was, like the virgate, one quarter of the master unit, or 60 acres. Presumably this note was necessary because, as suggested above, the local name slipped into depositions by accident? Later at Little Chart we find the entry "defends itself for three sulungs, now for two hides", which, when compared with the same entry in Domesday Monachorum[29] repeats this tax evasion in sulungs alone. We can now see how the hides slipped into the text. The solution to the area of the sulung was always there to be read, in plain sight! These are the eleven words remaining to complete our twenty: just twenty words in perhaps two million which ultimately raise the dead.

Of course, by 1066 let alone by 1086 some shires and even smaller places had come to view the hide rather differently, as I have already said. It had once been an omnibus unit so that in the Tribal Hidage, a document apparently (in part) pre-dating King Alfred's reign, the sum of all of England's 34 shires can be converted from hides to make-up a total of 24 million acres, which covers an area we would today measure at 23.396 million acres.[30]

The later created Danelaw shires, of course, those shires distinguished by the Peace of Wedmore as non-English shires, could only count in carucates, that is in arable land (land already broken to the plough) after their creation, for Danish settlers had no idea what a hide might be, but then their failure to count all lands or surfaces did not matter, not until 991. In that year the creation of a tribute called danegeld linked land to taxes (gelds) for the first time, at which point the hidated shires found themselves penalised for their surveying efficiency because the Danelaw shires were only admitting to tax-possession, or liability, of part of their territory.

This inequitable superimposition of systems, which was certainly appreciated by many English stewards, men now serving new, Norman, masters after 1066, made it essential for the Crown to discover some better yardstick of productivity than land-holding. This it did in the succeeding century. Domesday seems to have served both as an audit of tax evasions and as a means of assessing the extent of the commuted, the "black" (as we say now), economy, all the failures to pay full taxation. The new taxations of a century later were revised to include money. This Domesday superimposition is, however, useful to us for it resulted in all shires, not just Kent, exhibiting individuality in their selection of unitary combinations in 1086. For us the great bonus is that no-one was editing or standardising the evidence given, it was all set-down just as the men on the spot spoke it and, as a result, it now provides us with regional, cultural and economic evidences that are not to be found in later documents of more homogenous construction.

CHAPTER TWENTY-THREE

The Characters of Counties in 1066

Each shire, it seems, had its individuality or "character" in 1066-1086 through its choice of units and meanings, though the common use of certain units for various land-uses also allows us to map "blocks" of affinities, relationships, across several shires.[31] We cannot expect to commonly encounter "extents" outside East Anglia (of course) and, similarly, not every county was hidated, nor indeed did every wapentake or hundred in a given shire invariably employ identical patterns of logic when selecting units.

So in Essex we find that the total area, or acreage, of this hidated shire was aggregated in Domesday Book at 957,330 acres, which we can compare with the 961,800 acres recorded in 1848. The hidated Chelmsford Hundred, landlocked and in the middle of the shire, returned 86,800 acres altogether, which in 1875 was 86,650 acres. On the other hand the peninsular Dengy ("Witbricteshern") Hundred in 1086 not only counted her acres of land (all uses) in hides but also counted her foreshore and the salt marshes beyond, mud beyond the limit of habitable land, just as the Admiralty was still doing in 1786. The reason for this – well, even in 1786 there was no Ordnance Datum by which to set the bounds of land and sea.[32] Hundredmen in 1086, just like Nelson's navy, also had to decide for themselves where the one ended and the other began. We can say that as practical peasants those living inland saw things rather differently from those living on, or near, the coast. However we should note that the overall picture of Essex as a hidated shire, in spite of such practical problems, was exemplary.

In 1086 Middlesex was still a rural shire for London, though a valuable city, was somewhat confined, being mainly within the "square mile". She "enrolled" a shire hidation of 212,054½ acres and this is 95% of a more recently surveyed area of the shire at 223,500 acres. Surrey (including Southwark), on the other hand and other bank of the Thames, enrolled 485,850 acres in 1086, or 104% of the area recorded for the shire in the late 19th century. Each of these shires counted their woodlands in a different way, one side of the river one way, the other in another. Moving up the Thames, in Berkshire woodlands were expressed in three different ways, according to the hundred involved, and yet another group of hundreds here made no woodland entries at all! Here there were "forest" entries and we can suspect possible "forest" in the details given for others. (See map 2) Meadows she expressed in five different ways with (once again) none entered at all for one hundred. (See map 3) As already explained, this did not mean that such assets did not exist, simply that they were subsumed under another land use.

"A century hence the student's materials will not be in the shape in which he finds them now… villages and hundreds… will have been reconstituted and pictured… this history of land-measures and of field systems will have been elaborated. Above all, by slow degrees the thoughts of our forefathers, their common thoughts about common things, will have become thinkable once more". These words were penned in 1897 by F.W. Maitland at the conclusion of his book, "Domesday Book and Beyond". His prophesy was only a few years out, I think, though I fear some people may not want to see it fulfilled?

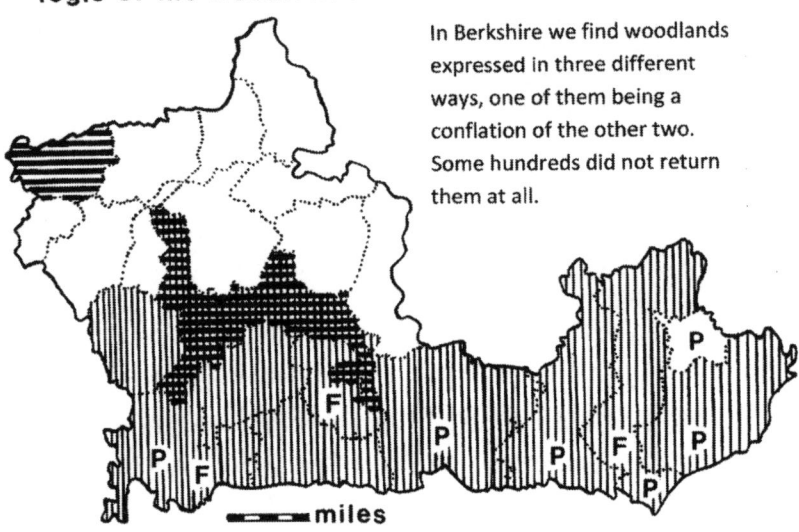

BERKSHIRE in 1086:
logic of the woodlands

In Berkshire we find woodlands expressed in three different ways, one of them being a conflation of the other two. Some hundreds did not return them at all.

BERKSHIRE in 1086:
logic of the meadows

In Berkshire we find the majority of hundreds carefully recording their precious meadows and for this five different formulae were employed.

The Characters of Counties in 1066

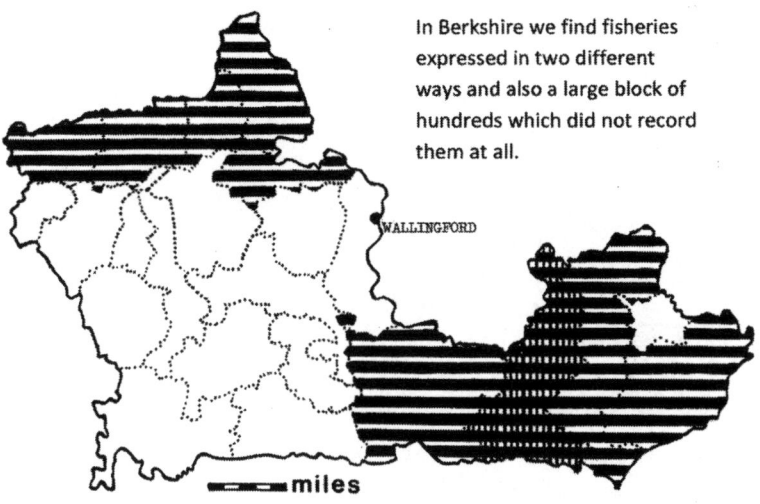

BERKSHIRE in 1086: hundrethal logic of the fisheries

In Berkshire we find fisheries expressed in two different ways and also a large block of hundreds which did not record them at all.

CHAPTER TWENTY-FOUR

Ploughlands

When we look at the overall picture of ploughlands and especially the historic arable, as counted in 1066-1086, and then convert the totals for each county to acres, we discover a surprisingly consistent picture of tillage when laid against the reconstructed, or aggregated, total areas of each shire. While Derbyshire and Staffordshire only tilled 10-20% of their Pennine shires many counties were ploughing in the range of 40-60% by 1086.

What is even more surprising, when we compare these percentages with those made in 1875 we find, with the exception of London in Middlesex, that such later totals perform <u>consistently</u> alongside those of 1066-1086, though these two sets of figures are separated by eight centuries! Whether we look at 1066-1086 or 1875, it seems that English national tillage (as defined by land actually under the plough) did not then subsequently recover and did not even expand until 1953-1954, by when the Second World War had made exceptional demands![33] This is not what we have been told to expect, though (of course) we know nothing of comparative yields, per acre and shire, at each date.

If men were generally ploughing almost as much land in 1066-1086 as in 1953-1954 then there must have been a very good reason for it, but it has not been remarked before. It seems to tell us of the national emergency caused by a succession of invasion attempts between 1068 and 1084, confirming that there was indeed a need to sustain large defence forces against such repeated attempts. What is more, the population was then much smaller than in 1875 or 1953, so the effort made was (in national terms) supreme.

We can say that by applying consistent units we have achieved consistent statistical validity and also made some surprising discoveries, discoveries which need to be more closely investigated.

COMPARISON OF TILLAGE ACREAGES, 1086-1955

This table shows the actual ploughs at work (at 120 acres per plough), in each of the shires named, converted to a percentage of each shire's area. The final column shows the area of each shire given-over to all agricultural uses in 1953-55, including tillage. The influence of WWII is obvious.

COUNTY	1086 as %	1875 as %	1938 as %	1953-5 as %	% ALL USES AGRICULTURAL 1953-5
Essex	50-60	40-50	30-40[1]	40-50	ex – 70-80
Suffolk	50-60	50-60	40-50	50-60	ex – 70-80
Norfolk	40-50	50-60	50-60	40-50	ex – 70-80
Cambs	30-40	60-70[2]	50-60	70-80	ex – 80-90
Beds	50-60	40-50	30-40[3]	40	ex – 70-80
Herts	40-50	40-50	30-40[3]	40-50	ex – 60-70
Middx	30-40	0-10[4]	10-20	10-20	ex – 10-20
Surrey	30-40	20-30	10-20[4]	20-30	ex – 40-50
Kent	30-40	30-40	20-30[3]	40-50	ex – 60-70
Hunts	40-50	50-60	40-50	60-70	ex – 80-90
Northants	40-50	40-50	10-20[3]	50	ex – 90-100
Leics	40-50	30-40	10-20[3]	40	ex – 80-90

Rutland	50-60	40-50	20-30[5]	30-40	ex – 80-90
Oxon	60-70	50-60	20-30[3]	20-30	ex – 80-90
Berks	40-50	30-40	20-30[1]	30-40	ex – 60-70
Notts	40-50	30-40	20-30[6]	40-50	ex – 70-80
Derbs	10-20	10-20	0-10[6]	20-30	ex – 60-70
Staffs	10-20	10-20	0-10[6]	20	ex – 70-80
(AVERAGES	38-48	34-44	23-33	37-44	67-77)

1. Considerable urban expansion
2. In Cambridgeshire there had been extensive fenland reclamation
3. Considerable urban and industrial expansion
4. The expansion of Greater London
5. Urban and reservoir developments
6. Considerable urban, mining and industrial development

CHAPTER TWENTY-FIVE

Could a Plough, Plough So Much?

The question inevitably arises, "would a plough in 1066-1086 have invariably tilled 120 acres in a year"? That is the standard we require for consistent use of our carucate units, so did men at the time expect as much? Is and was this a reasonable expectation around which to build a unit?

Of course some soils are easier to till than others and no doubt tillage practices also varied, as did yields. We cannot presume any sort of common, universal, husbandry though some historians have done as much. There were no agricultural colleges to enforce standard practises and methodology, no vehicles of communication in which to disseminate knowledge or ideas. We can, I think, presume that husbandry methods varied just as widely as did the choice of units by which to measure areas, each locale with its own practices and traditions and, just maybe, long experience had taught the tillers of the soil in each locality the best practises for local conditions. We should not automatically and arrogantly dismiss the practical wisdom of generations of the peasantry.

How many "yrths" (ploughings),[34] "earths" in Thomas Tusser's words, were bestowed when land was "broken for barley",[35] or how many passes were "stetched" for anything else, in any place, we just do not know. How many times it was necessary, or desirable, to cross-plough a field or a strip in any shire is elusive. William Cobbold in c.1910 spoke of five earths for winter wheat in Suffolk but we cannot even implant his world, certainly not his equipment, on our Domesday peasantry.[36] Besides, soil quality and type are nowhere consistent, even in Suffolk.

The purpose of the Domesday plough-totals was, we should remember, to provide a rule-of-thumb check on increased profitability of estates; "if more can be had" was the King's instruction and I think he intended both geld and provisions. No-one was making an agricultural efficiency survey or calculating soil quality against resources. As far as we can tell (using consistent unitary values) this rule-of-thumb was accurate for its purpose. Walter of Henley[37] even claimed that 160-180 acres were possible in a year with the men working for 250 days out of 365, "thanks to holy-days and other encumbrances". Yields, of course, fall outside the art of ploughing, but anyway there was in 1086 no way of checking on output, only on motive-power units.

We see many entries where the ploughs at work were fewer in 1086 than the historic total had been, which meant fewer acres were being ploughed than the 1066 entry of arable land, with the accompanying laconic remark, "and more are possible". England clearly believed that she needed all the resources she could muster in 1086, both for provisions and also, in taxes, for defence purposes and the only means of estimating profits was by counting ploughs. Under such conditions the intelligent agronomist would have incentive to raise yields, though the most common likely result of such pressures would be soil exhaustion with correspondingly lower yields for years to come. The reduction in plough-totals also tells its own story, confirming the deleterious effect on agriculture of successive invasion attempts by various coalitions of brigands and foreign armies, for that was indeed the real history of King William's reign.

CHAPTER TWENTY-SIX

Areal Units

1 HIDE = 240 ACRES   1 SULUNG = 240 ACRES

1 VIRGATE = 60 ACRES   1 JUGUM = 60 ACRES

1 CARUCATE = 120 ACRES = ANNUAL/HISTORIC
TILLAGE = 8 BOVATES

1 BOVATE = 15 ACRES

1 PLOUGH/PLOUGHLAND = 120 ACRES
ESTIMATED TILLAGE (A CARUCATE)

1 ACRE = 22 X 220 YARDS = 4 X 40 PERCHES

1 ARPENT = 1¼ ACRES
(A French unit usually applied to vineyards in Domesday Book)

For out of olde feldes, as men sey,
Cometh al this newe corn fro yeer to yere;
And out of olde bokes, in good fey,
Cometh al this newe science, that men lere.
(Geoffrey Chaucer "The Parliament of Foules")

CHAPTER TWENTY-SEVEN

Occluded Evidence: Other Land Uses

As I have said, each shire in Domesday Book displays its own "character", a phenomenon dictated by the understanding or definition men had or made of certain common nouns, also by their local application of a particular unitary noun, especially in the pastoral sector. Another influential factor was the dishonesty of the local tenants-in-chief, for as they had most to pay so they had most to gain by evading the geld. What happened when they did was that their own free sub-tenants (subinfeudations) adopted the same moral standards as their lords. It is noticeable that the very minor freemen were the most honest of all when it came to paying taxes, they had neither "good lords" nor considerations of "blood" to protect them from the law. At this time (and for long afterwards) "blood", that is birth, claimed privileges when brought before the law.

Apart from the essential grazings for the oxen who pulled the ploughs, and their winter feedings of meadow hay, there were other specialised estimates to be recorded. Omnibus areal (square) measures, like hide and sulung, might well incorporate ploughlands and ploughed land, when honestly applied, but they were also important as historic records in those suspect and dishonest cases where these plough units had been misused in order to reduce geld liability, by reducing declared areas (much as the ploughlands and the Anglian "extents" were used for audit purposes in other shires), allowing the Crown to check the sum total of all land, whatever use was made of it. This was because the obligation to pay the geld, as I have said before, lay upon the land. Geld was a land tax as well as a specie-only tax. Landowners were liable for it, not their "penny-less" land workers. If something had been recorded in the past ("in money or in orf") it should still have been there in 1086, it could not just disappear! Moreover, "if more can be had", was the King's instruction, he certainly did not want to hear of less!

Geld was a specie-only tax, so only those in the money economy could pay it. Subsistence peasantry were not part of the money economy, they gave services and "in kind" to their landholder or lord instead and he (or she) decided whether to consume or to sell the produce received from their local peasantry. The peasant's small, individual, outputs could never normally hope to reach the high value that was the silver penny. It took a lot of eggs to make a penny basket, unless you were a battery farmer!

Now, both the linear and the areal units could be used for those topographies locally defined as "meadows", "pastures" or "woodlands", with smaller areas (such as the valuable water-meadows) defined in acres. We do also find tiny woods at times, expressed in acres and not just for the record but because they were specialised and valuable woods. In Gloucestershire at Westbury on Severn (f.163) we find a very great rarity entered, a "firwood" and at Chilwell and Easton in Nottinghamshire (f.289v.) we see, along with four acres of "underwood", a four acre "willow plantation".[38] At Dartford in the Axton Hundred of Kent we have mention of an alder slade taken from the King's estates by a former sheriff! However, a large group of shires did not measure their woods and underwoods in these linear or acre terms at all, but instead in terms of swine, and these have also occasioned much discussion in the past. We need to examine these entries for they were and are, also, units of measurement and not just vague and hopeful guess-estimates. There were no pointless inclusions in these surveys, everything was quantifiable.

CHAPTER TWENTY-EIGHT

Swine Renders and Swinewoods

In some shires we are told of swine-renders, so many swine given in exchange for the right to agist pigs, usually on wood-pastures though pigs will root in many places and "wood" does not have to mean "trees". Unless otherwise informed I think we can take these to be a tithe, that is one pig rendered for every ten kept, with entries of other ratios (when these are given) as notes of exceptional practise. In many other shires, however, they speak of "swinewoods", woods for so many swine, and these appear to be units of woodland which could be open to pigs but not necessarily, or ever, representing real pigs. At times whole areas are reckoned in this way at two acres per pig. Occasionally we see a more circumspect employment of words, "woodlands swine can graze" or "not for grazing" and these make the point for us. Pigs can be great destroyers of underwood and coppice, though very useful for clearing woodland floors. In coppiced woods it would be essential to keep all grazing animals out until the coppice-stools had regenerated sufficiently to withstand browsing.

Many scholars have made the mistake of talking of "pannage" and "pannage woods" when interpreting such "swinewood" entries as these, pannage being the feeding of swine on beech-mast and acorns. Such talk has certainly confused historians and students alike. "A great many figures can have been no more than approximations", claimed one scholar with what he called "swine farming" often "obviously round-number estimates"[37] If that was the case, if this was in his view their only food and all-year-round agistment we should ask what the poor pigs were going to live on outside the short-lived pannage season, for beech-mast and acorns are an autumn phenomenon! No, the inevitable conclusion is that these swinewood statistics are <u>units</u> of woodland which may, or may not, have been agisted by swine. These are <u>not</u> pannage woods, in fact, for beach-mast and acorns only fall <u>once</u> in a year and in some years <u>not at all</u>, so the poor pigs would certainly starve to death in any year! If these represent anything more than a unit of woodland measurement it is as agistment, as year-round feedings, for (in fact) swine will root and clear bracken and brambles in a most efficient manner. Swine-woods do not necessarily mean swine and they do not have to mean oak-woods, they are units of woodland, they are acres. Two acres of agistment should feed a pig for a year, independent of pannage, and any sort of rough cover will suffice for nourishment.

In Sussex the swine-renders seem to have been so variable that they were often entered specifically: one in seven, one in three, even one in two! Maybe the pork and bacon business was booming, thanks to the industries of the Weald?[39] Well, someone in Suffolk, Sussex and elsewhere had a market for pig products. In the Babergh (Two) Hundred of Suffolk pig-keeping declined between 1066 and 1086, with a corresponding increase in sheep-keeping, so in this case ground may have been deliberately cleared by the swine in order to create safe pasturage for the sheep.[40] In Surrey there were pastures rendering one in seven or one in ten pigs, but there were <u>also</u> swinewoods, "woods" measured at two acres per pig. The use of <u>both</u> units tells us that <u>only one</u> of them referred to pig food while the other referred to acres, an interesting local separation and confirmation.

The validity of this two-acre unit is conclusively proved in Surrey where we encounter the "Surrey semi-sus" ("silva de CL porca et dimidia"),[41] the equal of Maitland's "Bedfordshire semi-bos" ("et ibi est semibos"!).[42] Of course there were other entries like this for other things, for in Essex we encounter "homo dimidius" and in Cambridgeshire "dimidii villani"![43] Whilst these men might, in reality, have enjoyed some peculiar social status and the labour of the plough-ox might have been shared with a neighbour I think the "half-pig" can only represent a one acre total of woodland.

In Aylesford Lathe in Kent the swinewoods generally fall into a sequence, thus 2, 4, 6, 8, 10, 12, 16, 20, 40, 46, 50, 60, 70, 80, 100, 120, 140, 200, 230, 300. We can hardly claim these to be random, odd corners of estates, they much more resemble planned enclaves of woodland. In Middlesex we see swinewood totals displaying remarkable dimorphism, each according to their hundreds, and there were six hundreds in all.[44] There is much to be learned from the study of such constants and such variables.

The use and distribution of all the several woodland units among the many shires we have examined is also interesting. The Midlands and the North mainly used linear calculations, with the exception of Lincolnshire, which relied on acres. It is still the least wooded shire in England. The West Country used both linear and acre units, the South-East mostly relied on swine-renders, but in the East and stretching across to the leafy Chilterns they employed swinewood units.[45] These variations seem to reflect the relative values of woodlands in their shires, which in turn reflect the tightness of local definitions, relatively woodless Lincolnshire being a good example of tight definition because all woodlands had a high valuation in this shire.

CHAPTER TWENTY-NINE

The Values of Woodlands

The local value set upon woodlands, as in Lincolnshire, seems to have affected the minimum quantities of acres recorded in each shire though, of course, population pressure would also be important. Buckinghamshire, as a well wooded county, ignored anything less than 32 acres whilst Norfolk, Suffolk and Hertfordshire started at two acres. The upper limits of areas were rather more consistent at 4,000 acres though both Norfolk and Suffolk had no woodlands larger than 2,000 acres. In the swine-render shires, where one pig will still represent two acres, we commonly start at 10 acres but only Kent goes as high as 5,000 acres. Darby suggested that this entry, under Wrotham, near Sevenoaks, was possibly situated in the Weald, but as this (greensand and ballast geology) area of Sevenoaks was not recorded by name at all before the 13th century, it was probably heavily wooded even in 1086. As for Lincolnshire, her precious woodland resource ran from one acre to only 1,000 acres maximum.

The linear-unit shires also started low (at 1, 2, 3 or 5 acres) with the exception of Warwickshire. However they rose rather higher to 16,000, 24,000, 32,000 and 36,000 acre blocks and Worcestershire rose to 112,000 acres, but their exact definition of "woodlands" was not so precise as in the swine-wood shires and clearly included intermixed woods <u>and</u> pastures of various qualities. The group of shires which made use of both linear and acre units (together) for woodlands displayed a similar pattern: Dorset and Devon commenced at half-acre woodlands but linear applications covered massive areas of mixed topography. Wiltshire, in one entry, listing a 96,000 acres maximum clearly intended Salisbury Plain, a very mixed habitat.[45]

Remember, "woodland" may include hunting grounds of various kinds, or sources of fuel, rather than trees. Clearly we are often looking at managed landscapes, for in every place there needed to be some restrictions on the browsing of potential fuels as well as nice distinctions made between underwood and timber. In Cornwall the linear totals rose to 32,000 acres, but here the "underwoods", presumably the most valuable woodland parcels, ran only from one to 60 acres.[47] We have already dealt with Cornwall's most interesting mineral-rich areas, which involved something other than woodlands. Nottinghamshire's acre-unit woodlands must have been valuable for they ran from one to 50 acres and Dorset's from half an acre to 40 acres. Once again these reflected relative values and (presumably) special local treescapes, assets of more than usual value, trees rather than fuel.

Up against the, rather fluid and dangerous, Welsh border units became jumbled, probably as a result of incomers taking-over abandoned estates. There were single linear units, swine-woods and many indefinable "heys". These "heys" do not seem to embody any precise value, they were clearings of some sort. In later venery they came to denote killing grounds for game flushed from cover and, so, many may at this date represent game-rich enclaves, we might say "parks", though (of course) not "emparked". We see similar generalisation in the Weald where they said "denes" when actually hiding the true extent of the Weald and its industrial resources. We are told of several Worcestershire "forests", or places where forest law (game laws) ran, and among such coincidences were the

Malverns, a landscape not exclusively noted for trees but still with mixtures of both cover and open terrain offering excellent hunting, so that it eventually became royal forest, known as Malvern Chase. Here, near to the Welsh borders of England and then up into Shropshire, we have a sort of buffer-zone exhibiting disunity of terms, a mixture not found in the Mercian shires to the east. And speaking of evidence for older kingdoms, Lincolnshire also stands out as the ancient Kingdom of Lindsey.

CHAPTER THIRTY

Sheep Pastures

Swine were, of course, ubiquitous, raised for pork and bacon, both the peasant's own, anonymous, pig and the larger (demesne) entries we actually see recorded, but sheep pastures are only sporadically entered and only in some shires, where they seem to have represented industries other than mutton-production. Apart from their great value when folded on arable land sheep also provide fleeces for spinning and weaving and, in season, milk for cheese-making, so (like swine) we might expect to find them agisted in woodlands or on marshes as well as on arable or pasture lands. However, they are not such hardy and indiscriminate omnivores as swine.

Sadly Darby chose to accept Round's assertion that in Essex sheep represented cheese-making flocks actually detached as berewicks on Canvey and Foulness Islands. Neither place is mentioned in Domesday Book and the evidence from the 16th century, on which Round based his assertion, is misleading.[48] In fact in Essex the real sheep, the flocks actually recorded in 1086, were distributed right across the shire with the largest flocks inland or on estuarial grazings. Some were even in north-west Essex.[49] These flocks seem to have been the essential suppliers for the woollen industries recorded in Domesday Book all along the north Essex and south Suffolk border area and whilst there were many modest flocks there were also some large (commercial) enterprises, the largest (at

810 sheep) being well inland at Hanningfield.⁵⁰

So, it is not only sheep pastures, reckoned at one sheep per acre, that we should be looking at but also the flocks of sheep if we want to obtain a picture of agriculture. Many other potential grazings for them were probably encompassed under the general "pasture" entries. At West Walton in Norfolk we find a large flock adjacent to the marshes and fens of the upper Wash and there are other sheepwalks in the Guiltcross Hundred, on the Norfolk-Suffolk border, in the East and West Flegg and Walsham Hundreds and in Lothingland in Suffolk.⁵¹ The Brecklands and even Dunwich carried sheep though there were few kept on the Sandlings.

But if flocks are specifically mentioned, we should probably incorporate them into our aggregated areas, at one acre per sheep, as they represented commercial activity of one sort or another occupying a part of the landscape which may not have been recorded in detail elsewhere. Recording them satisfied the need to verify land-holdings but it also complied with the instruction, "if more can be had", for whether as meat, milk cheese or wool, sheep represented profit and also resources for war, and they could be fed on many and various topographies in season, though for marsh-feedings transhumance would be essential.

CHAPTER THIRTY-ONE

Marshes and Fens

Sometimes these are entered in Domesday Book in linear units and (of course) when they are, they present no problems. Thus at Langtoft and Baston in Lincolnshire we find (respectively) "marsh two leagues by two leagues" (16,000 acres) and "marsh 16 furlongs by eight furlongs" (1,280 acres, or two square miles). However, at Marham and Clackose in Norfolk we are told that the ordinary "extent" of the place was "one league and a furlong by half a league and a furlong" (2,310 acres) but adding "and the marsh measurement is unknown". These extents sound as though they represent "wallings" along the line of the Ouse, as they did at West Walton, so the "marsh" mentioned was presumably salting beyond the seawall, subject to periodic inundations? Unlike those of the Dengy Hundred of Essex these peasants were not counting low-water for their imaginary datum, they were more risk-averse.

Fens, of course, involve waters and, indeed, the fine line to be drawn between marshes, salt-marshes or saltings, washes, fens and foreshores is far from certain, even today. My published proposition that the eel-rents of the Fens and the fisheries which were entered in Domesday Book might be indicators of fenny or open waters, with four eels to the acre of water and one penny to 70 eels, has caused much jocularity in the past among scholars, yet at Wisbech in 1086 we can say that there were 4,000 acres of farmland recorded with (by this method of estimation) 12,000 acres of waters and fenland, some 16,000 acres in all, and in the 1930's the whole of this fenny hundred was estimated between 16,300 and 16,700 acres, the town itself (by then) comprising 4,600 acres of this total.[52] Again, at Downham in 1086 a woodland and two fens together totalled 695 acres; in 1251 two "marshes" and a little park together totalled 700 acres in the same place.[53]

Of course when we are given the value of a fishery it is difficult to know how many fish, or acres of waters, this might represent. In Suffolk at Blythburgh, Dunwich, Beccles, Worlingham and Willingham they gave "renders" of herrings. Herrings, of course, are pelagic and the vessels concerned put out to sea, so we are not estimating the area of the Dogger Bank but instead their catch as a fishing fleet. The total "render" in 1066 had been 112,000 herrings but in 1086 it was 142,000. If this represented a tithing of the catches made then we are looking at a total "harvest" of about one-and-a-half million herrings! At Beccles the render doubled whilst Blythburgh fell from 10,000 to 3,000 herrings but with the addition of a new 50/- rent. Now, if this rent actually represented commutation, then here we have an indicator of roughly 12 fish to the penny. I suggest that this rent represented something other than the humble herring (at such a premium) and maybe they were cod? This would certainly explain commutation, the change in rent, from in-kind to cash.

In Huntingdonshire (f.205) the fisheries of the Abbot of Ramsey were worth £10, those of the Abbot of Thorney £3 and those of the Abbot of Peterborough £4, presumably on the Rivers Ouse and Nene: respectively $2,400^d$, 720^d and 960^d. Whether these sums jointly represented nearly 49,000 fish each year is impossible to say. At Alwalton (f.205) the fishery which rendered 1,000 eels may have been a tithing but it also paid 60^d, which might indicate a catch of fish as well as eels and lampreys? The extensive fenlands in the north of this shire are the obvious resource of all these fishermen, including the resource (then in existence, but now lost) of Whittlesey Mere.

At Colne, Holywell and Warboys (fs.204, 204v) there was "marsh", the largest (Holywell) measuring 4,000 acres, but for the most part the fenlands seem to have been the fisheries and the Abbot of Ramsey may well have had rights over thousands of acres of terraqueous appurtenances. At the famous Whittlesey Mere in 1086 we can use Domesday Book's figures to propose about 3,000 acres of land and over 5,000 acres of waters. By 1800 this was returned as 3,950 acres with 4,050 acres of land and water, as the once famous Mere (now sadly destroyed) was gradually eaten away in the succeeding centuries.[54] So in 1086 it was about 8,000 acres in all, <u>as it still was</u> in 1800, but the balance between land and water had shifted. At Wisbech, in the Fens, as we have seen, in 1086 there were 4,000 acres of farmland and 12,000 acres of waters and fens, 16,000 acres recorded all-in. By the 1930's the town itself was said to comprise 4,600 acres and the whole of this fenny hundred was between 16,300 and 16,700 acres.

In Nottinghamshire at Gringley-on-the-Hill (f.286v) the render from the Trent was 1,000 eels, which if we allow a standard unit of four eels per acre would be 250 acres of waters (fishing rights) "rendered". Elsewhere we seem to have 70 eels to the penny and in Shropshire they measured eels in "sticks" of 25.[55] In Berkshire, in the Wyfold Hundred, we see fishing rights blanketing some 23 square miles over an area assessed as the same number of square miles today, whilst in the Ganfield Hundred we see rights over 25½ square miles covering an area now assessed at 25.125 square miles. In this whole shire some 14.5% represented fisheries whilst in Oxfordshire only 2% of the area concerned fishery rights.[56] I can only suppose that in some shires fishing rights encompassed all the streams of a given topography whilst in other shires men tied such rights specifically to the larger open waters of rivers or to meres.

CHAPTER THIRTY-TWO

Validating the Evidence: Preferential/Beneficial Hidation

In the past a great deal has been made of the proposition that some places and estates were given some form or other of exemption as "beneficial hidation" and the concept is now deeply inscribed on both memories and in text books though, in fact, it never existed in principle at all. It was the result of a mistaken belief that these surveys were measured (on-the-spot) directives issued by supermen, rather than being, in reality, gatherings of verbatim evidence and opinions from the local inhabitants which were then compounded, conflated, with historic records.

Because scholars never appreciated the audit nature of Domesday Book, with its novel principle of checking one set of records and one process of recording against another, because they never realised that pre-existing records were incorporated alongside freshly deponed (local) evidence, because they accepted that the surveys and circuits must have been measured on-the-spot by an educated elite, because they never realised that the geld was both a land-tax and a specie-only tax, for all these "good reasons", the only possible solutions to the arithmetical dilemmas involved seemed to be to claim both the application of beneficial/preferential hidations and the incompetence of the clerks taking-down all these statistics on-the-spot.

These canards were particularly easy for historians to believe because contemporaries, especially "Norman" noblemen, so obviously believed that "tax relief" should be possible. Some apparently believed that they were entitled to it, because they followed the foreign custom of contributing treasure only when their overlord required it and so had no concept of a regular, regulated and specie-only taxation. After all, this was only to be found in England. Other landholders seem to have found unilateral actions a convenient means of reducing the irksome pre-existing (geld) hidations and (geld) carucations, whilst the Church had a doctrinal aversion to paying taxes based on both ancient historic precedent and on Cluniac doctrine.[57]

Moreover the problem was not just wilful disloyalty, at the time to be counted as treason, but it stemmed from the earlier accession to the English throne of two non-English Kings, men who had no idea how English finances worked, let alone of the structure of English political and social machinery. Both Cnut and Edward (the Breton) had been foreigners and so they never understood their own, inherited, tax system. To them it was simply the icing on the cake of kingship. There was also the principle that the Crown does not tax itself, because taxes are raised for the benefit of the Crown. Lands that had once been "terra regis" but which subsequently changed hands, sometimes had never paid geld for their "worth" before 1086! Prior to 1086 no system existed by which to check payments, they were all "on trust".

So, at Wimborne Minster we find that the place had always been "terra regis", royal estate, so the entry says, "it is not known how many hides are there because it never paid geld T.R.E.", a statement of fact, though in fact it contained 45 ploughlands (5,400 acres of historic arable). No-one had ever asked the locals what it measured and it had not been included in 991 because it was Crown estate. Of course the King would tallage his lesser tenants here, who would generally pay in-kind (being only subsistence farmers), but as most of them were not land-holders (freemen) they were not liable for the geld and probably could not have paid it anyway for lack of markets and of volume. The land-holder was the king and the Crown does not tax itself, though it can sell or retain the produce and revenues of its estates, just like its chief tenants.

If we look at Southwell in the Thurgarton Wapentake of Nottingham we see the geld duly paid on demesne carucates – that is 2,700 acres of geld paid for 22½ carucates (which had become 24 ploughs by 1086 and so actually owed it on 2,880 acres) – land distributed among freemen – undertenants who were the archbishop, soldiers, clerics and Englishmen. However, another 23 ploughs were also at work here and at a total of 47 ploughs this now comes to 5,640 acres under cultivation. These landholders were therefore, not paying for their peasant under-tenants, who did all the work and kept them supplied! Perfectly logical to them no doubt, why pay for the peasant's land? Well, because the geld was an obligation which lay upon the land and so upon the landholder, not upon its cultivators.[58] And note that we are not even looking at all the land-uses involved, not at a total estate or a comprehensive "hidation" involving all assets (as the English would define it), we are (in fact) only looking at the arable land, for this place had once, for a time, been a part of the Danelaw and only the English really understood the underlying principle of hidation.

If we can excuse such cases (undoubtedly the Crown would not have done) there were nevertheless very many cases of blatant dishonesty . At Lechlade in Gloucestershire Siward Bairn claimed six hides, all exempted by the late King Edward, "for which he could show the King's seal"; Edwin the Huntsman (f.50v) only paid for one virgate on the two hides given to him by King Edward. Why should King William now honour such claims, even if they were honest? The Shoyswell Hundred of Sussex in its entirety had managed to avoid <u>all</u> gelds and in two entries (f.19 and 19v) we are therefore told that this whole hundred "has never paid geld". How convenient for the Count of Eu, its new landlord! At Carshalton in Surrey Geoffery de Mandeville went a step further for he took five manors and made them into one, simultaneously <u>reducing</u> his geld from 27 to three and a half hides, though both the men of the shire and the men of the hundred (the local juries) deponed that they had never seen the writ or the livery officer giving him seisin from the King! This was an audacious piece of arithmetic, reducing all five estates to one and that the lowest valued (former) single entry and it was apparently accomplished in total absence of a legal title if, as we are told, he did not even have seisin of these manors!

Large and even small, the cavalcade of such tax evasions is endless for the simple reason that no-one had ever audited the geld returns and some estate stewards must have been as inventive as modern accountants. Peter de Valognes claimed that Harkstead in the Samford Hundred-and-a-Half of Suffolk was a berewick of Brightlingsea in Essex, one comprising a mere five acres, though it had 38 tenants and 1,200 acres of arable! At Melton Mowbray Geoffrey de la Guerche deponed a jumble of units which came to 1,715 acres but the Domesday clerk dryly entered "in each hide are fourteen and a half carucates" and when we recast and apply this formula and then also compare it with a list of all the berewicks dependent on Melton Mowbray (including meadows and woodland), we amass almost 12,300 acres, 19 square miles of land, which then actually accords with modern surveys of all the places named to produce the identical area.[59]

Of course, when royal demesne lands were let they were then gelded, or should have been gelded according to their hidation, for undoubtedly many had been measured at some time in the past before the geld had been linked to hidation. If they now escaped the geld-rolls that was because they had been ancient terra regis or because the earlier records had been lost before hidation had been so linked (in 991). Holy Cross (St. Leofrey's) and Battle Abbey were both noted as having paid no geld since they had received their lands from the King – a slip on the part of the royal clerks at work in the 1070's! Presumably there was no precedent for re-assessment prior to 1085-86?

At Great Bromley Ralph Pinel had given his dues directly to the Crown's officers instead of giving them through his overlord, Geoffery de Mandeville. This is interesting in another way. Whatever his reason for doing this, by so doing he had usurped his lord's authority and title to the lands, because Ralph was not himself a holder in-chief ("in capite") but an under-tenant of Geoffery's.[61] Minor freemen paid their overlords and this, of course, conveniently left scope for abuses by the overlords. Letting them make direct payments would suggest that their overlord may have been manipulating his free tenants' liabilities, as an entry in the Dialogus de Scaccario was to detail and confirm a century later.

In the Kingsclere Hundred of Hampshire Edwin the Huntsman held two hides given him by King Edward, "then as now assessed at one virgate". Were they really given in perpetuity? It was worth a try! At Micheldean in Gloucestershire three thanes held two hides and two and a half virgates, though on these 610 acres they really had 10½ ploughs at work (1,260 acres tillage), and "King Edward assigned these lands exempt from geld in return for (these thanes) having custody of (his) forest." Well, these thanes seem to have taken custody of more than the grant originally given to them as verderers! The saintly King also granted favours to young ladies who had "fed his hounds". At Down Ampney, Ednoth held 15 hides of geld but King Edward had remitted the geld on five hides. "In Oakington (Cambridge, f.202) the wife of Boselin de Dives holds one and a half hides which the Bishop of Bayeux delivered to her but the men of the hundred do not know on what grounds"! How circumspect of them. Whatever former kings had done, surely the half-brothers of present kings were entitled to do?

Chippenham in the Staploe Hundred of Cambridgeshire (f.197) "was assessed at 10 hides (T.R.E.) but a certain sheriff reduced them to five hides, by permission of the same King, because its "ferme" (payment) was a burden on him, now it is assessed at five hides". The recording clerks were not fools and what we need to realize is that Ordgar was not only the sheriff concerned, he was also the holder of these hides and so liable for their geld!

Time and time again we see tax-evasions and corruption recorded, and recorded (and maintained) both before and after 1066. In Cheshire, for example, there were many evasions by chief lords and at times we see these boldly annotated by the royal clerks, for these new records were, in fact, secret reports to their "mandarin" (chief clerk) and the clerks were the King's own men. Cheadle was hidated at 1,441 acres but the recording clerk noted 2,880 acres in all: the supervising "commissioners" ("legati") were presumably too ignorant and indolent to understand his written report. In Lancashire we hear of estates claiming that they were not only quit of geld but also of the fines for bloodshed and rape! Do we believe such claims, any of them? Well, it was not the business of the clerks to correct their betters, only to set it all down for the king's information! At Okehampton in Devon Sheriff Baldwin claimed that he only had three virgates and a "ferding" (or quarter virgate) T.R.E., only 195 acres, but the King's clerks recorded that 30 ploughs could till this estate!

Rather more boldly, Miswell in the Tring Hundred of Hertfordshire (f.138) "was assessed at 14 hides T.R.E. and now at three hides and two and a half virgates – yet there are still 14 hides", said the recording clerk. These men were not creatures of the Church, subject to abbots and bishops, able to be suborned by powerful lords, these clerks were the King's own trusted servants and they knew their business and their duty. They also knew their place when dealing with their "betters". I think these CAMERARII were brave men, good and loyal servants to the Crown and the man who directed them and to whom they reported, their "mandarin", was a genius.

CHAPTER THIRTY-THREE

The Lesser Domesday: A Senior Partner

"The special treatment of Essex, Suffolk and Norfolk, which gave them in far greater detail than the remaining thirty-one shires of the Domesday folios, has been explained by many scholars as "an incomplete edit". While the "greater" Domesday contains 382 double pages this "lesser" Domesday actually contains 450 double pages and these for only three shires! Why should they be so different? Indeed, how can we speak of a "lesser" which is physically larger than the "greater"?

To explain this disparity scholars have argued that King William's untimely death cut short the editing process, which had already been applied elsewhere, in order to reduce the "original" mass of details collected to manageable form. So (they argue) the "lesser" set of folios must represent some formative process left "unedited". We should ask ourselves why this should have been when <u>the whole purpose of the surveys</u> was to collect details and correct facts? Was there a sudden shortage of vellum? Why should the king's death interfere with the editing process? Was the whole process now to be abandoned as a great "white elephant"? Was it all now thrown in a corner and forgotten? Surely the king did not personally compile these folios?

Perhaps even more surprising is the proposal that (as we have been told) someone edited the "greater" volume after voluminous notes had been compiled, for if these survey teams actually did measure every acre, all in six months, a truly incredible achievement, how could they have then edited their findings as well? Think about it, if the original gatherings for the "greater" Domesday were pro-rata with the "lesser", then the original "rough notes" would have amounted to something like 4,650 double pages! How many clerks would have been required in the remaining twelve months between King William's departure for France and his death to précis, check, edit and engross such a colossal undertaking, yet a single clerk edited these supposed "4,650 double pages"? And had he achieved so much, then surely he could have taken one more month in which to process the remaining three shires?

Of course, <u>none of the Domesday folios</u> were implemented before King William's death in 1087, there just was not time in these few months to engross the circuit returns in the fair copy we see today, let alone run a revised geld. Had the fact-finding nature of the surveys ever been appreciated this would always have been obvious. Instead it was presumed that the Norman supermen were imposing surveys and order on the stupid peasantry! It therefore follows that the logic of this "accepted" argument is at fault: if the other folios <u>were</u> "edited", then why did the royal clerks not complete their task? They certainly continued to work for William "Rufus", the protests at his "avarice" make this perfectly clear, he was the first king to impose the findings for they were assuredly not ready before 1087. The answer is simple: the "greater" Domesday is in one form for one purpose, the "lesser" Domesday is in another form for a good reason, that is for <u>another</u> purpose. There was a special reason for the inclusion of so much additional detail and, <u>once again,</u> Domesday Book itself actually <u>tells</u> us the answer to this riddle.

The answer is in the colophon to the whole collection, which is found <u>not</u> in the main group of folios, not in the "greater", as one might expect, but instead it occurs (let us say appropriately) in the "lesser" Domesday. It tells us the year in which these surveys were made and then it goes on to say, "thus was made this DESCRIPTIO, <u>not only</u> through these three counties here but <u>also</u> throughout those elsewhere". This is quite explicit, "as made (or exampled) here, so elsewhere"! Using the simpler statistics enrolled in the "greater" Domesday, it is saying, it is possible to be equally accurate. Moreover there is more than duality of meaning in "DESCRIPTIO" for it can mean "a map", "a diagram" or "a written description" but also, most importantly, it implies <u>measured</u> evidence. In the "lesser" Domesday the measuring is evident, especially in the "extents" but also in the accurate hidation of Essex, and these three shires embody the systems of both the carucated and the hidated shires found elsewhere, <u>and</u> also (for good measure) the system of measuring by linear units. The lesser Domesday is most unlikely to be either a pilot or an afterthought for it emphasises the methodology to be applied throughout and to be applied to every folio.

"Facta est ista descriptio. Non solum per hostres comitatus. Sed etiam per alios"

In order to alter the meaning of this colophon and make it conform to their own theories experts have even gone so far as to say that its author was not competent in the Latin tongue! So, they claim, the "alios" should really have been "ceteros" in order to make the sense change to "all the others". Well, the meaning of *"sed etiam per alios"* is "those elsewhere (set out) in another place or way". The author knew what he meant and he was leaving a guidance note to his posterity. Those who came after him would need to know how this document should be read, this is the paradigm, though exactly <u>when</u> he came to this decision I cannot say.

I think we can call the "lesser" Domesday a mentor or book of instruction by which to apply the mass of information in the "greater" Domesday – an enchiridion. Yet the single scribe who engrossed the "greater" Domesday and put it into standard format put the "key" to unlocking the mystery of the units, the "twenty words" we have seen, deep in the "greater Domesday". Without the one the other was unfathomable.

Now some scholars maintain that seven clerks or scribes between them copied-out the "lesser" Domesday, basing this on minute differences of "hand" in the script employed. Whilst I agree that four or five different "hands" are displayed these need not be individual scribes. Would the three shires involved have required so many different scribes, all exceptionally educated and qualified (as we have seen); surely the entire survey did not employ 78½ exceptional linguists and mathematicians!

Yes, there are different "hands" but, as I have already observed, the standard training for all clerks was to copy the document in front of them, an exemplar, down to the last detail. That is why we sometimes see the perpetuation of mistakes, ancient mistakes reproduced in the scriptorium when books were copied, for copying was an over-riding discipline. Scribes were trained to be just like photocopiers. We can see the incorporation of earlier documents in both of our Domesdays by the curious variations in capitals and ligatures. My own assessment is that the same (senior) clerk, camerarius, wrote-up both the "greater" and the "lesser" Domesdays and in so doing he automatically reproduced distinctive features contained in the exemplars he had consulted, along with all the minute details. There was nothing amateur about the Anglo-Norman exchequer and chancery and if secrets are to be kept, then access to information needs to be carefully restricted.

As the DIALOGUS DE SCACCARIO says, "the exchequer is a sort of inner sanctuary of mysteries when everyone's books are opened and the gates shut..." Here sat Master Thomas Brunus, "at the head of the fourth seat", who kept a privy roll of royal secrets and prerogatives always in his charge and with him wherever he went, and his personal scribe did not, "sit with the other scribes but above them and overlooks the scribe of the treasurer"... "he is also called in with the magnates to all the grand matters of the exchequer".[61] Almost a secret service!

We have indeed been dealing with state secrets, we have finally succeeded in raising the dead.

CHAPTER THIRTY-FOUR

Presenting the Case: Summary of Findings

THE HIDE – a unit of 240 acres. A unit unique to England, <u>one not known elsewhere in Europe</u> and so totally alien to the incoming Norman-French. Along with three other unique units it is <u>the proof</u> that whoever wrote-down the findings of these surveys not only had to be adept (fluent) in three languages and arithmetic, they also had to be either English or English trained. It is most unlikely that <u>any</u> of the senior clerics or noblemen who oversaw this project (the legati or "commissioners") had such a range of skills and knowledge. Maybe this is why the value of the hide unit is clearly stated in one place – a needle in a haystack – one that only an exchequer-trained clerk could either find or understand!

    Because it is a unit unique to England (and perhaps because it became something of a state secret) we do not know the origin of the hide. The story of Dido and the hide of a bull, found in Virgil's "Ænid", would seem to be the likely origin.[62] My own estimate is that a very skilled thong-maker, working on a reasonable size bull's-hide, <u>could</u> just possibly create a thong ("rope") capable of enclosing 240 acres. This unit was originally employed as a comprehensive measurement of land, whatever the use made of that land, but this usage gradually changed and was corrupted c.1000, after it had been linked to assessment of the geld, for it then became inconvenient to great lords.

VIRGATE – a quarter-hide unit, its name is thought to be derived from O.E. "gyrd landes", possibly related in some way to the "rod" or perch (see below),[63] or perhaps to the custom of servile tenure "to hold by the rod"? Four perches make the width of an acre, another example of division into four parts.

Yet as a "fourth part" ("ferding") the virgate is sometimes employed as a linear, rather than a square, unit, and these two should not be confused: in which case it is a quarter of an acre's <u>length</u> (or "shot"), viz. 55 yards (10 perches).

THE ACRE – usually envisaged as a strip 22 x 220 yards (40 x 4 perches). The name is thought to be derived from O.E. "Æcer" or "aker", an open field, and has relations in Norway, Sweden, Iceland, Holland, Germany and Normandy, the root apparently being the Latin "ager" (land or field).

THE PERCH (or ROD) – a length of 16½ feet, usually (fancifully) attributed to the length of an ox-goad. A quarter of the width of an acre, hence "rood-land" and probably a standard surveying rod in England. Others have proposed that it could be either 15 or 18 feet, but our 16½ is their median and the difference in practise is very small. In fact the Old French perch was equal to 18 pieds or 19 English feet, so it seems that our insular unit was smaller than the French unit and, of course, that allows it to fit into our system of units more accurately: 40 perches = 1 furlong, 20 furlongs = 1 league.

THE SULUNG (or SOLIN) – a unit of 240 acres, a unit not only unique to England but a name unique to Kent. Difficult to identify the derivation which could either be Latin "solum" (soil, land) or "solium" (seat, rule) though Darby suggested the Old English "suhl", a plough.[64] Why it was only employed in Kent and only occurs after c.1066 alike remain a mystery as before this the shire seems to have been officially measured in hides. I think it was a purely local noun only recorded because in 1086 it was (for the first time) directly deponed by locals and the recording clerks, of course, had no powers to alter the evidence given.

THE JUGUM – a quarter sulung of 60 acres, once again not only unique to England but unique to Kent. The origin seems obvious by consultation with Varro and Columella: the square actus was "120 x 120 (Roman) feet and when doubled forms a iugerum... from the fact that it was joined" (Columella, book V). The Roman iugerum was, therefore, 240 x 120 feet, usually interpreted as 28,800 square feet or two-thirds of an acre.[65], so the meaning of "jugum" is either from the Roman unit or from the oft-quoted "yoke" (of oxen), as Columella says, joined (yoked) together. In terms of an eight-ox plough-team which could plough 120 acres in a year, 60 acres would represent two pairs (yokes) joined together, half a carucate (the unit of eight oxen in team together).

Incidentally, the "usual" size of the iugerum (28,800 square feet) is based on the Roman "pes monitalis" but the "pes drusianus", which was more commonly found in Britain (13.1 inches), will give a result of 4,800 square yards, which is much closer to the area of an acre.

THE CARUCATE – a unit of 120 acres, a unit apparently widely distributed and understood right across Europe, whose origin was obviously in the "caruca" or plough. As detailed in the text, it was an area that could easily be ploughed in the average year using eight oxen (stotts) to the plough.

It came to prominence in England with the Danish occupation of northern and eastern English shires during the ninth century when it displaced mensuration in the pre-existing hide units, though residual traces of both hides and (English) hundreds can be found in many such shires even in 1066-1086. Commonly used to assess the land traditionally under the plough, the established arable of any vill or estate, it is often found stated as "land for (x) ploughs".

THE BOVATE – one beast, one eighth of a plough-team, a unit of 15 acres.

THE PLOUGH TOTALS – of the same value as the carucate, actual ploughs were recorded because they provided the revised picture of arable exploitation by 1086. Either the arable had increased or decreased and in the event we often find qualifications (observations) such as "wasted" and "another plough possible" or some formula (apothegm) indicating blatant tax evasion. A very important audit check: "is it more or is it less than the record we already have?" Once again, "if more can be had".

THE LEAGUE – a linear measurement equivalent to 2½ miles, 4,400 yards or 20 furlongs and probably aggregated in furlongs, as miles are rarely mentioned in Domesday Book. The Old French "lieue" was equal to 840 French perches, or three English miles, but like the English perch, our league units were slightly smaller.

The test of this unit is that it can invariably be checked against later measurements (such as miles) whenever like-for-like comparisons are possible.

THE FURLONG – a linear measurement of 220 yards or 40 perches. Later references to the "acre shot" tell us the origin, the long side of a 220 x 22 yard acre strip. Occasionally we see it employed to express an area, when so many furlongs make so many acres. It is possible that it was sometimes employed as a vague reference to the run of a plough but in Domesday Book it is clearly used quite precisely and as a unit.

THE ARPENT – a distinctive French and Norman measurement of small area usually associated with viticulture. Older French sources have given it 1¼ acres, though some modern sources prefer 1.6 acres and in Canada it equals 10 French perches. Only rarely does it intrude for uses other than vineyards in 1086, and then, typically, when small French or Norman tenants did not understand English units and so they spoke their (foreign) minds.

THE GELD – a unique, an English, specie-only taxation invariably calculated in sterling (high silver content) coin, usually estimated in pennies: so many pennies on the hide. Because a silver penny had a high purchasing power such specie was beyond the mass of the subsistence peasantry who, anyway, often had no access to markets. The geld lay as an obligation upon the land and it was paid by landholders, that is by those who were "free" men. Freemen, of course, had defence obligations and so had to be able to purchase arms, which made it essential for them to be in the money economy.

This geld, or danegeld, began in 991 A.D. with the decision to pay a national ransom to Viking raiders, though it was not the first "tribute" ever paid. To make equitable assessments possible it was linked to pre-existing hidations as a land-tax and so it then continued as "so much on the hide", though in the carucated shires, where hidation had disappeared, it could then only be tied to carucates and we sometimes hear of "carucages".

As an "emergency" payment, originally an expedient, geld obviously could not be an in-kind payment (as court fines were) and so the peasantry had to produce in-kind in order to enable their landlords to market produce for specie. Foreign lords (like Normans) were more used to giving "contributions" of treasure, when required, and so this specie-only tax may have been unique in Europe (and one of the great attractions of England to brigands).

Its defect, by 1086, was that it could not take account of commuted (cash) payments, so the Domesday surveys paid special attention to such payments and then added valuations as well to their list of auditing questions. Not surprisingly, subsequent taxations gradually changed to money assessments so that gelds, hidations and carucages then disappeared. The new system of taxation that evolved in the succeeding century focused on wealth generation rather than land-holding alone, thereby closing the tax loop-hole of commutation.

CHAPTER THIRTY-FIVE

From the Crypt of History: A Monster or a Priceless Treasure?

Now that we no longer have a set of mouldering remains hidden in an obscure place and awaiting resurrection, but a living and breathing marvel in Domesday Book, how should we view it and how will Academia view it? Now that it is no longer some arcane and obscure mystery which the average student will not be able to comprehend without expert guidance, now that anyone who cares to can follow the units and paradigm to prove much more than the guesses which used to be presented as "facts", will it be welcomed?

We can run through our fingers, so to speak, this wonderful World Heritage treasure-trove but is its discovery either credible to, or welcomed by, others? Should it be accepted or should such knowledge and evidence really be suppressed? So many historians have repeated the "conventional view" of Domesday, the one presented by "dead authorities", though simultaneously calling for some greater insight, but <u>will</u> they now acknowledge that the evidence they always said they sought <u>has</u> been found, or will they rather deny that scientific methodology has any part to play in historical detection, will they deny that the words we have now seen in plain view have any relevance? When so many scholars have been frustrated in their search for a definitive and provable solution is it credible that such a solution has now been found? And, as always, when an answer has been found to some difficult problem and the methodology revealed, will it just be dismissed as "always obvious"? Do historians have the courage to face the truth?

What Domesday Book now has to say is that the world of 1066-1086 was a very different one from the words and pictures in our history books so that we have been teaching children falsehoods! Now we have a clear view of a far more complex English economy than we ever supposed before and we also have a tremendous amount of detail about agriculture and agricultural practises. We have a detailed and comprehensive picture which we can even add to the more recent revival of interest in peasant agriculture.[66] The Norman political scene has been transformed by what we have learned and it enables us to fit into place pieces of information from elsewhere, from other documents, things we never understood, just like completing a jigsaw puzzle.

What is also of importance is the cultural picture that emerges. There are some who see the Norman Conquest as completely divorced from the esoteric study of Domesday Book, to them the Book is an irrelevance, merely another illustration of the superiority of those "supermen" invaders who were both fitted and destined to win over an "inferior race". Instead of a lesson in the supremacy of violence, terror and ethnic separation we now see, instead, the triumph of cultural fusion in creating a medieval society that was to take its place in the centre stage of European kingdoms. And above all we see that instead of a brutal invasion delivering a superior culture (which was always a contradiction) we can now actually understand how the invaders were civilised by the society they had inherited.

It has always seemed to me that those who favoured the (so called) "Norman Conquest" and those who regretted it (for, as they saw it, the ending of the idyllic "Saxon" kingdoms) were both alike, in their worship of force. The one believed that success followed the "supermen" and the other believed that defeat was accomplished by such "supermen", and all believed that brutality, terror and violence were the way to create a kingdom of importance. When humanity cannot find a solution to some military success it always elects for a "master-race" mentality, with cold-blooded ruthlessness triumphing over "the weak", and a belief that might was right also helped to build a Victorian empire! The fantasy world of such "supermen" created by Victorian novelists and scholars further supported the Victorian (and later) English class system by elevating a Norman-founded aristocracy to a naturally superior race of leaders and governors. The proposition that only the Church had the learning necessary to conduct any sort of bureaucratic exercise and, in so doing, leading native peasantries into the paths of righteousness and enlightenment, is itself a colonial doctrine. Clearly such beliefs are now seen as pernicious and also inimical to social cohesion. I think they should no-longer be promoted. They have served their temporary purpose.

What Domesday Book has to say about the invasion of 1066 is also a revelation, especially when combined with the evidence of the Bayeux Tapestry. The detailed surveys of Sussex entered in Domesday Book for 1066 and 1086 help us to firmly establish that there was a fifth column at work for William, at Pevensey in 1066, for these surveys clearly reveal those estates which subsequently suffered heavy requisitions and a "demilitarised zone" and those who were (instead) rewarded for their co-operation.[67] A similar economic and topographic review is possible for the (so called) "harrying of the North", so that we can see that this was neither indiscriminate nor was it mindless and universal destruction.[68] It was an inevitable outcome of 20-30,000 men fighting one another over a limited area during several winter months.

Thus in "raising the dead" we have begun to discover positive attitudes in ancient local communities, also pragmatism and the ability to create and educate even in the absence of formal, didactic methodology.[69] In this there should be lessons for the future, for the world that will now replace everything we ever knew. We can now see how ridiculous it was to propose that on the one hand "Norman" nobles were brutal illiterates but yet, on the other, that they were also cultured and numerate because they measured and recorded the whole landscape of England – and accomplished this in six months! Such contradictions were founded on the Victorian belief that there can be no knowledge without universal (and approved Christian) education so that the peasantry must have been fools! Similarly we can dispense with the foolish contradiction that after systematically slaughtering a large part of the English peasantry, in a reign of terror, these conquerors still had an abundance of agricultural produce for themselves. And, of course, the question that was never answered because it has never been asked, how could a tiny invasion force subject to campaign deaths, disability and disease continue to replace itself and counter massive foreign invasions for twenty years if the English were always enemies, always in revolt and even denied weapons for defence?

It is, of course, also implausible that the whole area of England was measured as a "national grid" in 15 foot squares, even if it was accomplished during the course of four hundred turbulent years, by monks and priests. If it was, then where is the evidence for such an archive or for its preservation and consultation by the Domesday commissioners? Why does Domesday Book record so many regional variations if a standardised survey was employed? The use of such grids for high status sites of limited extent is a possibility, based on a very limited statistical base of just over one hundred sites, but what is not likely is the transformation of the English countryside![70]

Raising the Dead

In Norfolk <u>alone</u> we have the evidence of alternative surveys from <u>five times as many sites</u>.

Our history of this period, it seems to me, was hijacked a century ago in order to serve and bolster colonial practises and a social model which is not relevant today. There is nothing new about "historical revision", it has always been the case that the facts of history have been interpreted, or even suppressed, in order to gratify the political elite of the moment, and that is (after all) what history was originally created for, to tell people <u>how</u> to think! Yes and it is still being employed in this way in this particular field of study in order to sustain intensive agriculture (among other things) in the face of peasant agriculture and agroecology, even though socio-political emphasis has metamorphosed.[71] Consequently we have permitted both the perpetration and promotion of an historical pastiche which surpasses Piltdown, a betrayal of generations of children and students who looked to history for factual content and the means of discovering some way of creating a better future. We have condemned them, as we have also been condemned, to repeat the mistakes of the past. If we now wish to redress this wrong, we certainly need to choose a new future – and this time we need to "do it right".

More than a century ago academics chose to ignore rational academic enquiry and to opt instead for a "quick fix" which would be politically acceptable. Today scholars are understandably reluctant to admit this or to stand up and defend dogma which they were compelled to believe. They do not wish to disinter the body or uncover the skeleton in the cupboard, they would rather that statistical validity was silenced and censored. But this is to deny the whole validity and importance of the Domesday Surveys with their incorporation of earlier records. Domesday Book is <u>not</u> irrelevant to the Norman Conquest, it was and is the foundation stone of our English Medieval Kingdom and of our constitutional history for without it there would not have been, could not have been, Magna Carta.

On the other hand, surely it is best to pretend that such a discovery was never made? Surely it would be best to continue with the fantasy history we have always had and which has been lovingly crafted to inform our ignorance? It is, after all, so comforting. Should we now "raise the dead" or should we "leave the dead to bury the dead"? That perhaps is the question? Should we continue to seal the grave – to seal it for ever and in the hope that artificial intelligence will <u>never</u> be able to reveal such an act of cowardice? Ah, but what if one day it does!

APPENDIX

Actual Linear Measurements Entered in Domesday Book – Converted to Acres

FURLONGS x FURLONGS = ACRES

½ x ½ = 2½ 　　　　5 x 4 = 200
1 x ½ = 5 　　　　　6 x 3½ = 210
1 x 1 = 10 　　　　　2 x 11 = 220
2 x 1 = 20 　　　　　6 x 4 = 240
1½ x 1½ = 22½ 　　8 x 3 = 240
2 x 1½ = 30 　　　　5 x 5 = 250
3 x 1 = 30 　　　　　7 x 4 = 280
7 x ½ = 35 　　　　　5 x 6 = 300
7½ x ½ = 37½ 　　　3 x 10 = 300
2 x 2 = 40 　　　　　8 x 4 = 320
3 x 2 = 60 　　　　　5 x 7 = 350
3 x 2½ = 75 　　　　6 x 6 = 360
3 x 3 = 90 　　　　　5½ x 7 = 385
5 x 2 = 100 　　　　5 x 8 = 400
4 x 3 = 120 　　　　6 x 7 = 420
5 x 3 = 150 　　　　5 x 9 = 450
4 x 4 = 160 　　　　6 x 8 = 480
4½ x 4 = 180 　　　7 x 7 = 490

Presenting the Case: Summary of Findings

$$6 \times 9 = 540 \qquad 7 \times 11 = 770$$
$$6 \times 10 = 600 \qquad 8 \times 10 = 800$$
$$8 \times 8 = 640 \qquad 10 \times 10 = 1000$$
$$6 \times 11 = 660 \qquad 6 \times 18 = 1080$$
$$7 \times 10 = 700 \qquad 9 \times 13½ = 1215$$
$$8 \times 9 = 720 \qquad 10 \times 13 = 1300$$

LEAGUES X LEAGUES = ACRES

½ x ½	= 1000	
1 x ½	= 2000	
1½ x ½	= 3000	
1 x 1	= 4000	= 6¼ square miles
2 x ½	= 4000	= 6¼ square miles
1½ x 1	= 6000	
2 x 1	= 8000	= 12½ square miles
1½ x 1½	= 9000	
2½ x 1	= 10000	
2 x 2	= 16000	= 25 square miles
3 x 2	= 24000	= 37½ square miles
4 x 2	= 32000	= 50 square miles
5 x 2	= 40000	= 62½ square miles
6 x 2	= 48000	= 75 square miles
5 x 3	= 60000	= 93¾ square miles
4 x 4	= 64000	= 100 square miles

ANOMALOUS DECLARATIONS

2 acres x 1 virgate = (2 furlongs x ¼ furlong?) = 5 acres

8 furlongs x 8 virgates = (1 x ¼ miles!) = 160 acres
(Kelham, Notts)

8 furlongs x 14 virgates = 280 acres

16 furlongs x 74 virgates = (2 milesx74 v.) = 2,960 acres
(Kelham, Notts)

9 furlongs x 50 virgates = 1,125 acres

8 furlongs x 1 mile = (1mile x 1mile!) = 640 acres

One furlong = presumably, one acre?

"One hide less 5 feet" (Lathbury, Bucks) !!

FURLS X FURLS	+ PERC	=ACRES
2 x 1½	+5	= 32½
1	x30	= 7½
13 x (1?)		= 130?
5 x 4	+6	= 207½
7 x 5	+4	= 357
8 x 7	+11	= 582
8 x 8	+12	= 664
6 x 15	+13	= 919½

Presenting the Case: Summary of Findings

LGS X FURLS	=	ACRES
1 x 1	=	200
½ x 2	=	200
½ x 3	=	300
½ x 4	=	400
½ x 5	=	500
1 x 3	=	600
1½ x 2	=	600
1 x 4	=	800
2 x 2	=	800
½ x 10	=	1000
1 x 5	=	1000
1½ x 4	=	1200
1 x 6½	=	1300
1 x 7	=	1400
1½ x 5	=	1500
2 x 4	=	1600
4 x 2	=	1600
1 x 8	=	1600
1 x 10	=	2000
½ x 20	=	2000
2 x 5	=	2000
2 x 7	=	2800

Raising the Dead

LGS	FURLS	PERCS	LGS	=	ACRES
½	x 4	+ 3		=	407½
1	+ 2		x ½	=	2200
1	x 8	+10		=	1650
1	+ 3		x 1	=	4600
½		+ 20	x 1	=	2100
½		+3	x 1½	=	3022½
1	+1		x 1	=	4200
1		+100	x 1	=	4500
4	+2		x 2	=	32800
½ x		+1	x 1	=	2005

LGS	FURLS	PERCS	LGS	FURLS	PERCS	ACRES
1	+4			x9		= 2160
1	+2	+10	x1			= 4450
2	+6		x1	+4		= 11040
2½		+12	x1		+10	= 10185¾
2½		+15	x1½		+70	= 15994
1		+100	x ½	+1		= 2475
	6	+3		x 4½	+4	= 279½

LGS	PERCS	FT	LGS	FURLS	PERCS	FT	ACRES
2	+8	+5	x1		+12	+4	8164.6
½	+2			x4		+4	402.6
1	+10		x1			+4½	4051.4

Notes & Sources

1. H. C. Darby & I. B. Terrett, "The Domesday Geography of Midland England" (CUP 1954) p.433
2. H. C. Darby & I. S. Maxwell "The Domesday Geography of Northern England (CUP 1962 & 1977) p.437
3. Q.v. Arthur Wright, "Domesday Book Beyond the Censors" (2017) pps. 3-6 and chapters 2, 3 and 4
4. Ibidem p.16 quoting HITM 24031: Starke v. IRC (1995) STC 689
5. John Innes, "Domesday Book in the Classroom" (Phillimore 1982) pps. 14-15
6. Wright "'Fools or Charlatans' the Reading of Domesday Book" (2014): at Shalbourne, Burbage and Morton in Wiltshire the King's French servants used the French unit for meadowland when the rest of the shire used acres, elsewhere it is correctly applied to vinyards. I take my 1¼ acre unit from Devize, "La Vie de la Forêt Française Au Seizieme Siécle "(1960)
7. Q.v. Wright (2017), especially the distribution map on p.11
8. L. J. M. Columella's "De Re Rustica", trans Forster & Heffner (Harvard 1955 and 1979), Loeb Library
9. Oliver Rackham, "The History of the Countryside" (1986 and 1995) pps. 338-9
10. H. C. Darby, "The Domesday Geography of Eastern England" (CUP 1957) p.122
11. A. Davidson "East Anglian Archaeology 49" (UEA 1990)
12. Wright (2017) p.101

13. White's Directory for Norfolk, 1836; also Wright (2017) pps. 93-5 and map on p.97
14. Ibidem, pps.99-101
15. Wright (2014) pps. 362-4 and map on p.366
16. Ibidem, pps. 365-71
17. G. O. Sayles, "The Medieval Foundations of England" (1948 and 1966)
18. J. H. Round "Danegeld and the Finances of Domesday" in "Domesday Studies" (1888) vol. I, pps. 42-77
19. Arthur C. Wright, "English Collusion and the Norman Conquest" (Frontline, 2020) pps. 46-8 and 102-107
20. V. H. Galbraith, "Domesday Book and Its Place in Administrative History" (OUP 1974)
21. Darby and Terrett op. cit. (CUP 1954), Northamptonshire
22. Ed. John Morris. "Domesday Book" in "History From the Sources" (Phillimore, 1976-84)
23. Anne Williams, "The Victoria County History of Dorset", vol.III (1968)
24. Wright (2014), pps.83-4
25. J. H. Round, "The Victoria County History of Essex", vol. I (1908) pp.424 and 440; John Morris "Domesday Book" vol.32 "Essex", 3.16 and the editorial note; Wright (2014), pps.83-4
26. M. Beresford and J. St. Joseph "Medieval England, An Aerial Survey" (CUP 1958) pps.86-94 and figs.32 a-c and table 1
27. Q.v. Wright (2014) pps.272-4 quoting the "Dialogus de Scaccario"
28. Bede's "Historia Ecclesiastica Gentis Anglorum", chapter 25: several translations available
29. "Domesday Monachorum" of Christ Church, Canterbury, ms.E.28: sometimes claimed to be pre-and sometimes post-Domesday Book
30. Arthur Wright, "Hoax! The Domesday Hide" (2009) pps.51-2 and p.59

31. Q.v. Wright (2017) maps on pps. 11, 21 and 34
32. Wright (2014) pps.78-9, and 2009 the maps on pps.31 and 37, pps.29-36
33. Wright (2014) and table on p.93
34. "Rectitudines Singularum Personarum"
35. Thomas Tusser "Five Hundred Points of Good Husbandry" (1573)
36. Q.v. George Ewart Evans, "The Horse in the Furrow" (1960), p.130. I also recommend the practical good sense of Dorothy Hartley when explaining the wisdom of the peasantry, whatever the period concerned, q.v. "The Land of England" (1979) especially pps.90-91
37. Q.v. E. Lammond (ed.) "Walter of Henley's Husbandry" (1890): no more than 260 days of ploughing due to "holidays and other encumbrances". In Lombardy they reckoned 269 days, see C. Cipolla, "Before the Industrial Revolution, European Society and Economy, 1000-1700" (1976 and 1981). W. Abel gives a range of 250-270 days to a working year in "Agricultural Fluctuations in Europe" (UP 1986)
38. Rackham firmly maintained that at this date fir did not grow in England, q.v. Oliver Rackham, "The Illustrated History of the Countryside" (1994) p.44
39. Arthur C. Wright, "Decoding the Bayeux Tapestry" (Frontline 2019) pps.106-7 and 150
40. Wright (2017) p.58
41. Wright (2014) p.206
42. F. W. Maitland, "Domesday Book and Beyond" (1897) pps.179-180.
43. Q.v. Sir Henry Ellis, "A General Introduction to Domesday Book" (1833) vol 2; pps.428 and 441
44. Wright (2014), table on p.208
45. Wright (2017), map on p.34
46. Ibidem, p.36. The military zone on Salisbury Plain today covers the poorest soils and comprises 95,000 acres

47. Ibidem, table on pps.35-36
48. Q.v. Wright (2014) pps.381-4. Also Arthur Wright, "Cantles of Tart and Pungete: Cheesemaking in Essex" (2004)
49. Wright (2014), distribution maps on pps.383-4
50. Ibidem, pps.373-381, maps pps.375 and 384-9, maps pps.385 and 387
51. Wright (2017) p.94, p.100, pps.105-109
52. Wright, "Hoax! The Domesday Hide" (2009) p.98
53. Ibidem, p.99
54. Wright (2014) p.211
55. Ibidem, pps.55-6
56. Ibidem, p.218 and map on p.215
57. The problem of taxing the Church dated back to Constantine and was, in effect, an attempt by the Church to create tax-havens. Cluniac doctrine insisted on the physical enlargement of the Opus Dei, not on the diminution of those revenues which made it possible.
58. This is exemplified in the "Dialogus de Scaccario", q.v. Wright (2014) pps.271-2 (Crown v. Earl Robert of Leicester)
59. Wright (2014) pps.152-3
60. Ibidem pps.148-9
61. Q.v. W. Stubbs "Dialogus de Scaccario" (OUP 1870 and 1960); also D. C. Douglas and G. W. Greenaway "English Historical Documents, 1042-1189" (1953) vol.2
62. Q.v. W. Smith, "A Classical Dictionary of Biography, Mythology and Geography" (London, 1859)
63. "Oxford English Dictionary" (OUP, 1921)
64. H. C. Darby and Ella M. J. Campbell "The Domesday Geography of South-East England" (CUP 1962 and 1971), note on p.502
65. Which requires reconsideration in the light of the difference between the pes Monetalis (11.6 inches) and the pes Drusianus, the latter (13.1 inches) being reported

in more frequent used in Gaul and Britain: R. P. Duncan-Jones "Britannia" Vol.II (1980) pps.127-133.
66. Q.v. Prof. dr. Jan Douwe van de Ploeg "The Importance of Peasant Agriculture: a Neglected Truth" (2017)
67. Q.v. Wright (2019) pps.55-60 and 102-6
68. Arthur C. Wright, "English Collusion and the Norman Conquest" (Frontline, 2020) pps. 35-45
69. For a fuller and wider-ranging discussion of English cultural and educational attainments by 1066 see Wright (2019)
70. Q.v. "dico AE", 'dictionary of agroecology' developed by INRAE, La Région Occitanie" (for peasant farming).

Index

A

Abingdon Chronicle – 49
Acre – 11, 42, 67, 95
Areal units – 20, 37, 43-5, 49, 67
Agroecology - 104
Alwalton – 80
Arithmetical ingenuity – 4
Arpents – 28, 67, 98
Artisan hubs – 40
Audit – 35-6, 40, 47, 51, 53, 57, 97, 99
Aylesford – 32, 73

B

Babergh – 72
Baston –79
Battle Abbey – 49, 86
Bayeux Tapestry – 102
Beccles – 80
Bede – 55
Bedfordshire – 73
Beneficial hidation – 45-7, 50, 82-88
Beresford and St. Joseph – 49
Berkshire – 39, 59, 81
Black Economy – 57
Blythburgh – 80

Bottlebridge – 33
Bovate – 67-97
Brecklands – 78
Brightlingsea – 85
Buckinghamshire – 74
Burghal Hidage – 47

C

Cambridgeshire – 48, 51, 87
Canterbury –29
Carshalton – 85
Carucates – 46-7, 49-51, 56, 67, 96
Castle Camps – 48-9
Camerarii – 17, 87-8.92
Characters of Counties – 58-61, 68-70
Cheadle – 87
Chelmsford – 58
Chepstow – 51
Cheshire –46, 87
Chilterns – 73
Chilton Foliot – 32
Chilwell – 69
Chippenham – 87
Clackose – 79
Clerks (see Camerarii)

Index

Cnut – 83
Cobbold, William – 66
Colchester – 49
Colophon – 91-2
Colne – 81
Commutation – 80, 99
Comparison of tillage – 63-4
"Conspiracy" – 45-6
Canvey – 77
Cornwall – 39-40, 75
Cuttlestone – 29

D

"Descriptio" – 91
Danegeld – 51, 56
Danelaw – 51, 56
Denes – 75
Darby – 33, 74, 77
Darby and Terrett – 46
Datum – 58
Death of King William – 89-90
Dengy – 58, 79
Derbyshire – 40, 62
Devon – 40, 75, 87
Dialogus de Scaccario – 53, 92-3
Domesday Book – 2-4, 7, 11, 101, 104
Domesday Monachorum – 56
Domesday Surveys – 13-14, 104
Dorset – 47, 49, 75
Down Ampney - 86
Downham – 80
Dunwich – 78, 80

E

"Exchequer unit" – 44, 50
"Exempt Geld" – 45
Earths –65-6
Easole – 29
East Anglia – 34-6, 41, 58,
Easton – 69
Eastry – 29
Edward ("Confessor") – 83-7
Eels – 79-81
Essex – 58-9, 77, 79, 85
Extents – 34-6, 41, 58

F

"Ferding" – 95
"Fiscal hides" – 44-5
Farley's text – 47
Fens (see Marshes) –
Firwood – 69
Fisheries – 20, 35, 79-81
Flegg (East and West) – 78
Flood meadows – 33
Forest – 27, 39, 59, 75-6
Foulness – 77
Furlongs – 11, 42, 97

G

Great Bromley - 86
"Greater" Domesday – 54, 89-92
Galbraith – 46
Ganfield – 81
Geld Rolls/Geld – 45, 47, 49-50, 69
Geld unit – 44, 49-50, 98
Giddings – 49

Gloucestershire – 69, 84, 86
Golden Valley – 48, 50
Goostrey – 46
Gringley-on-the-Hill – 81
Guiltcross – 36, 78

H
Hambleton – 31
Hampshire – 86
Hanningfield –78
Hastings – 49
Herefordshire – 74
Harkstead – 85
Herrings – 80
Hertfordshire – 48, 87
Heys – 75
Hidation/Hide – 16, 43-5, 47-53, 56, 84, 94
Hollywell – 81
Holy Cross – 86
Huntingdonshire – 29, 33, 49, 80

I
Indemonstrable Hypothesis - 44
Inquisitio Comitatus Cantabrigiensis – 48

J
Jugum – 43, 55, 67, 96

K
Kelham – 37
Kent – 29, 43, 54, 74
King William's "folly" – 44, 47, 89
Kingsclere – 86

L
Langtoft – 79
"Lesser" Domesday – 54, 89-93
Lancashire – 39, 87
Land-inning – 35, 78
Leagues – 11, 13, 41, 97
Legati (Commisioners) – 19, 94
Leicestershire – 48
Letchlade – 84
Liber Eliensis –49
Lindsey/Lincolnshire – 73-4, 76, 79
Linear units – 10-12, 34, 41-2, 106-10
Little Chart – 56
London – 59, 62
Lothingland – 78
Lythe – 37

M
Maitland – 59, 73
Marham – 79
Marshes – 20, 79-81
Meadows – 18, 20, 32-3, 59, 69
Meanings of nouns – 18-24
Melton Mowbray – 85
Micheldean – 86
Middlesex – 59, 62, 73
Mile – 11
Minerals – 39-40
Miswell – 87
Morris, John – 47, 49

N
Newark – 37
National tillage – 62-4

Index

New Forest – 39
Norfolk – 34-5, 74, 77, 104
Norbury – 46
Northamptonshire - 47
Nottinghamshire – 31, 37, 41, 69, 81, 84

O
Oakington – 51, 87
Occam's razor – 10
Odstock – 32
Offlow – 28
Okeford – 49
Okehampton – 87
Oxfordshire – 39.81

P
Pannage – 71-2
Pastura ad pecuniam – 32
Pastures – 18, 20, 25, 30-1, 69
Pawton (Pydow) – 39
Peasant agriculture – 19, 23-6, 58-61, 65-6, 69, 104
Perch – 11, 14-15, 42, 95
Pevensey – 102
Phillimore – 47, 49
Piltdown – 104
Pirehill – 28
Ploughlands/Ploughs – 46-8, 62-7, 96-7
"Preferential Hidation" – 45-6, 82-88
Proof (of deponed evidence) – 37, 41, 72

R
Rhos – 29
Rhufonoig – 29
Robert of Rhuddlan – 29
Rollestone – 28
Round – 44-6, 49, 77
Rutland - 31

S
South Tawton – 40
Samford – 85
Sandlings – 78
Scortesbroc - 55
Sevenoaks – 74
Sheep pastures/flocks – 77-8
Shoyswell – 49, 85
Shropham – 36
Shropshire - 81
Silva minutae – 29
Silva pastura – 28-9
Sod-busting – 31, 51
Southwell – 84
Specie-taxation – 69, 98
Staffordshire – 62
Stanneries - 40
Staploe – 87
Stradlie – 48
Suddington – 48
Suffolk – 36, 66, 72, 74, 77-8, 85
Sulung – 16, 43, 55-6, 67, 95
Surrey – 59, 72-3, 85
Sussex – 85
Swine – 71-3, 77
Swine woods – 71-3

T
Tax Evasion – 51, 57, 68, 82-8
Terra regis – 83, 86
Thanet – 55
Thurgarton – 37, 41, 84
Tin-streaming – 40
Terrington – 35
Totmanslow – 29
Treasure trove – 2
Tribal Hidage – 55-6
Tring – 87
Tusser – 65
Tybesta – 39

U
Underwood – 31, 69, 75

V
Virgate (unit of area) – 37, 42, 67, 95
Virgate (unit of length) – 37, 42, 95

W
Wales – 49, 75-6
Walpole – 35
Walsham – 78
Walsoken -- 35
Walter of Henley – 66
Warboys – 81
Warwickshire – 74
Wasta – 46
Water-meadows – 33, 69
Weald – 75
West Country – 73
West Walton – 35, 78-9
Westbury – 69
Whittlesey Mere – 81
Willingham - 80
Willow – 69
Wimborne Minster – 83
Wingham – 29
Wirksworth – 46
Wisbech – 79-81
Woodland – 18, 20, 25, 27-9, 59, 69, 75
Wood-pasture – 30-1, 72
Worlingham – 80
Wrotham – 74
Wyfold – 81